WHEN GOD BREAKS THROUGH

WHEN GOD Breaks Through

JOHN AND
ELIZABETH SHERRILL

Tyndale House Publishers, Inc.
Wheaton, Illinois

Library of Congress Cataloging-in-Publication Data

When God breaks through—people change! / [compiled by] John &
    Elizabeth Sherrill.
        p.   cm.
    ISBN 0-8423-1129-7
    1. Christian life—1960-   I. Sherrill, John L.   II> Sherrill,
Elizabeth.
BV4515.2.W44   1993
248.4—dc20   92-36441

Printed in the United States of America

99 98 97 96 95 94 93
 8   7   6   5   4   3   2   1

Contents

When God Breaks Through

When God breaks into human experience, change follows! Do you and I play any part in this miracle-working process? Do we simply wait passively for his initiative? Or is there something we can do to allow his life-changing Spirit free access to our lives?

We believe there is a role for human beings to play in the drama of our transformation—a role so elementary that in our vanity we may neglect it. It is simply: to see. To open our eyes to his presence in every event, every individual.

"We know," wrote St. John in his first letter, "that . . . we shall be like him, for *we shall see him* as he is." Our destiny, the purpose for which we were created, is to arrive at the full stature of him in whose image we were made. As Christians we know this. Through hard experience we also know that no striving on our part, no effort of self-improvement, brings about this metamorphosis. It is the vision of God alone, the perception of him *as he is,* within and beyond and throughout his world, that works the change.

Like any other talent, the ability to see God is a skill that increases with use. The more we saw of God yesterday, the more he will show us today. The more we see today, the more he can reveal tomorrow, until at last, with St. John, we stand transformed before his unimaginable glory.

St. John wrote his letter to report his own adventure of seeing God, and Christians ever since have followed his example. Seeing God is not a solo effort undertaken in isolation. From the beginning, believers have shared with one another their awestruck or their intimate glimpses of his nature.

"Look!" we cry to each other, over the back fence or over the centuries. "Here's what he showed me today!"

Here is what he has been showing the two of us. Here are the places, the times, the people that have opened our eyes. We have glimpsed him in tragedy and triumph, in seasons of deep prayer and at moments when we least expected it. Indeed, if there is a single identifying mark of God, whenever we catch sight of him, it is surprise. He is never quite as we anticipated, never just in the spot where we saw him last. He is waiting for us this moment, in a form so new that only when we wonderingly perceive the difference in ourselves will we know that we've gazed into the face of God.

John and Elizabeth Sherrill
Chappaqua, New York
August 1991

ONE

GOD
Breaks
Through... As Love

It's said so often we may miss the marvel of it. God is love!

Could we have read that correctly? The force behind this awesome universe, the unimaginable power that threw galaxies into space—is love?

The mind cannot grasp so huge a concept; only the heart is big enough to take it in.

David

I hadn't seen David and Marilyn since they'd retired and moved to Arizona, but through Christmas cards I'd followed their ups and downs. For the past four years, since David was diagnosed as having Alzheimer's disease, I gathered that things had been pretty grim. Two months before a *Guideposts* assignment took me to Phoenix, Marilyn had at last placed him in a nursing home—and that's where she and I were driving now.

"He won't know you," she warned as she parked in front of the Spanish-style building. "He doesn't know the children, anyone."

It was true. There was no recognition in David's eyes as I gripped the passive hand on the arm of the wheelchair.

But he was obviously well cared for in this clean, cheery home. It was Marilyn I was concerned about. Nothing on her Christmas cards had communicated the strain on her of these last four years. She was down to ninety-eight pounds and badly stooped with arthritis, yet she was making the twelve-mile trip every day of the week to feed David his midday meal.

"This is Tib, dear," she told him for the fifth or sixth time. "Remember we used to be neighbors?"

No response.

"Who's this?" She lifted a framed photograph of their daughter from the dresser. David stared at it, then shook his head.

It was the same with pictures of their son, their grandchildren, their old collie. Marilyn lifted his hands from the chair arms, held them in both of hers, and leaned close.

"Who am I, dear?"

That same bemused stare. Then his face brightened. For just a moment he looked like the David I remembered.

"You love me," he said.

They were the only words he spoke during my visit. *But what else,* I thought, as the plane carried me back east, *do we need to know? About one another. About God.* When we don't know . . . when we can't understand . . . when we're not sure of anything at all . . . we can still say to him with joyful certainty: "You love me."

Elizabeth

The Secret

"Perfect love casteth out fear," wrote St. John, "because fear hath torment." Here is the story of a tormented man and the love that finally set him free.

One morning in April, Roy Baliles of Gastonia, North Carolina, saw two policemen walking toward his house. Instinctively he shrank back from the window, but the police strode up Gardner Street without glancing right or left. Roy sighed. Someday, he knew, the police would be coming—after him.

Roy Baliles, alias Roy Standley, was thirty-six years old, and for most of those years he'd lived with fear. As a boy he had often seen it on the face of his father, a farmer in the North Georgia mountains. He had seen it on his mother's face, too, and in the eyes of his five brothers and sisters. In the mountains, feuds existed; death and violence were the order of life.

Roy could not remember when he first began to carry a gun. It was as much a part of him as the fear; and the gun had caused the trouble.

One night when he was a lanky, rawboned fifteen-year-old, Roy was driving on a mountain road near his home when two men—one tall, the other fat, both dressed in civilian clothes—stepped into the headlights of his car. Roy slammed on the brakes. The men approached the car. In the headlights Roy saw a flash of metal.

The men were carrying guns.

Roy drew his own.

The fat man started to open the car door. In panic Roy fired. He fired twice before his gun jammed. The fat man crumpled to the ground.

Roy threw the gun down and prepared to defend himself with his fists. But the tall man straightened up from examining his companion. "He's dead. You're under arrest, boy. We're police officers."

The trial was held on December 16, 1936, in the little frame courthouse down the mountain from Roy's home. No consideration was given to the circumstances. The charge was murder in the first degree, the verdict, "guilty." Just after his sixteenth birthday, Roy was sentenced to life imprisonment in the Georgia chain gangs.

Life in the prison camp was grim. From morning to night Roy swung a sixteen-pound sledgehammer, breaking rocks on the road. Around his ankles were shackles, chained together so that he could not take a full step without faltering. After two years, chiefly because he was well liked by prisoners and guards, Roy was granted certain privileges. The shackles came off. After three years he was allowed to drive a bulldozer.

One morning during his fourth year on the road gang, Roy received word that his mother was ill. He was working his bulldozer several hundred yards from the main body of prisoners and guards. Beside the road was the prison pickup truck.

Roy stopped the bulldozer, climbed down, and quietly got into the truck. Then he turned the key, stepped on the

accelerator, and headed down the road. He wasn't particularly panicky; he just drove home to see his mother.

No one came after him. Yet immediately Roy discovered
that escaping prison had not set him free. More deadly than
official punishment, he learned, can be self-punishment. Each
hour at home increased his fear. He could not sleep or eat.
Forty-eight hours after his escape, he took off again. He
headed for Florida where no one would know him and
applied for work in the canneries.

"Name?" the man at the application desk asked.

"Roy . . ." Roy stopped. The man looked up, and Roy
made a quick decision. "Standley. Roy Standley."

"Yeah," said the recruitment manager skeptically, but
he put the name down, and Roy Baliles had an alias.

He worked in the canneries for two years, until his fears
forced him to get moving again. He was twenty-two years
old when he packed up his few belongings and headed north.
He traveled as far as Gastonia, North Carolina, where he
took work as a laborer at Myer's cotton mill. He did not
intend to stay in Gastonia, but after a few months something
happened that again changed his life.

Roy fell in love.

Working at the mill was a slim, brown-eyed girl named
Ella Bradley. Soon Roy knew he could not leave Gastonia
without Ellie. Each time they met, Roy considered telling her
he was an escaped convict, but somehow the right moment
never came.

The community welcomed Roy and his bride. Together
they bought a home, a brown-shingled house on Gardner
Street. The name on the mailbox read: Roy Standley.

Children came: a girl, then a boy, Sandra and Larry.
Roy settled down to the life of a model citizen. He was quiet,
steady, helpful to all. He was what the neighbors called a

"devoted family man." No one knew of the nightly prayers for strength to withstand the mounting torture of suspense. Many times in the middle of the night, Roy Baliles made up his mind to turn himself in. But in the morning, when the children crept into bed for a romp, he always changed his mind.

The war came. Roy joined the army and served for more than three years. When he returned home, he noticed that Ellie had something on her mind. "Who told you?" he asked impulsively.

"Your family didn't know it was a secret from me."

"You going to leave?"

"No," said Ellie. "I'm not going to leave, Roy."

It was easier now because Roy had someone he could talk to about the fear. But the suspense continued. The involuntary shrinking at the approach of police. The searching of faces for any hint that others, too, had discovered the secret.

"I wonder if anybody knows, Ellie," Roy found himself saying. "People are too polite, as if they're embarrassed for me." Ellie assured him it was just his imagination.

Then on April 13, 1956, twenty-one years after a fifteen-year-old panicked on a mountain road, authorities in Georgia received an anonymous telephone call: "Check with police in Gastonia, North Carolina. See if Roy Baliles isn't living there as Roy Standley."

Events after that moved swiftly. Three armed men descended on the brown-shingled house on Gardner Street. Roy saw them coming and broke out in a cold sweat. "Ellie," he called to his wife, "they've come." Then he went to the door.

"Come in," he said to the officers.

The police were surprised. "Why didn't you run?"

Roy turned and looked at Ellie, who was hugging Larry and Sandra to her for support. "I've tried that," he said.

"You can't run away, not really. From now on I'll put myself in the hands of the Lord."

Roy kissed Ellie and the children, then left with the officers.

Four days after his arrest, Roy Baliles was sent back to Georgia prison to resume serving his life sentence. It was over.

Except . . . up in Gastonia, something strange was happening. No one quite knows whose idea the petition was. Some say it was Ellie's. Others say it was the men at the plant. Still others believe it was the Gastonia police. Certainly the police and Roy's fellow workers were among the first to sign it. But it was Ellie Standley who went to the mayor, the chief of police, and the arresting officers, and got them to take the unheard-of step of signing a petition for Roy's parole.

Then Ellie stood on the street corner in front of the town hall and asked for signatures. For ten days neighbors cooked, ironed, and took care of the children. Ellie choked up when workers at the plant took up a collection and raised $130. "Just to tide you over, Mrs. Standley, until Roy gets back," they said as if they believed it.

A reporter on the *Gastonia Gazette*, Bill Williams, ran daily columns on the progress of the petition. The newspaper alone received 2,000 names. Each night Ellie added up the total. First it was 4,000. Then 7,500. Then 9,000. Atlanta newspapers picked up the story. Countless individuals and church groups began praying for Roy. Names poured in unsolicited. "We don't know Roy Standley personally, but how could this man really be bad?"

Within two weeks Ellie had more than 10,000 names. With the children, Bill Williams and her solicitor, Pat Cooke, Ellie took the petition to the Georgia Parole Board.

On May 3, 1956, only fifteen days after Roy was re-arrested, the parole board met to review his case. At noon of the same day, a guard came to Roy's cell. Other prisoners stopped talking; an unusual silence hung in the air.

The guard opened the door. "Why don't you go home, Standley?" he said. "You're on parole."

The story of Roy Standley is a classic example of the life-changing effect of a community's love. The petition was its dramatic, visible expression. But the love was there all along. Roy didn't know it, of course—not until the day after his release.

On that day, Roy went down to Myer's cotton mill, where he learned that his job was waiting for him. There he ran into a man who had worked with him for more than ten years. Roy spoke of his relief at being, at last, able to face his friends openly.

"It's an answer to prayer," Roy said. "It's like being given a new life, to have the secret out."

That's when he heard it. He was to hear it dozens of times in the next few days.

"Secret?" said his friend. "Why, you can't keep a secret in a small town, Roy. We've known it all the time."

John

Wamba and the Roofless Church

White men had killed his grandfather. Now he would kill to drive them from his land.

This is the story of a man, a church, and a struggle for freedom. This story took place in Kenya, East Africa. The man was once a Mau-Mau terrorist; the church was peculiar in that it had no roof. In these two, the ex–Mau Mau and the roofless church, is summed up the dilemma of Christians in the Third World today.

We met lanky, middle-aged Rebmann Wamba in the autumn of 1962 at St. Paul's Theological College in Limuru, Kenya, where we were holding a seminar on Christian writing. Wamba was a student at the college; he'd moved his wife and eight children to Limuru while he studied for ordination in the Presbyterian church.

Wamba was setting out on foot for the market as we finished our classes one afternoon, so we offered him a lift. The market was a happy confusion of shouts and bickering—except for the sudden silences that greeted us as we moved along the rows of stalls. We soon realized, however, that the narrowed eyes and hate-filled stares were directed, not at the intruders from America, but at Wamba—and this is what made us ask for his story.

When Wamba was a younger man, he told us, he'd been a leader among these same Kikuyu people. "They used to hasten to me when I came here to the market," he said in the slow and precise English he had learned in school. "I would talk much to them about the day my grandfather was killed by white men. My anger gave me heart-stirring words."

When the first talk of violent revolution against British rule—Mau Mau—was whispered by the Kikuyu people, Wamba felt he had found the movement that could free his people from domination by foreigners. He took the grisly Mau-Mau oaths, which bind men with black magic and horror.

The goal of Mau Mau was an independent Kenya, but to Wamba's amazement it encountered a hard core of opposition among his own tribesmen. These were Christian Kikuyu who objected, not to Mau Mau's aims, but to the savagery of its methods. These methods, however, the revolutionaries were sworn to. Traitors to the cause would be treated in the same way as the hated Europeans. The terrible toll of seven years' violent uprising against the colonial government was ten thousand dead—the vast majority not white people but Christian Kikuyu.

One night during this reign of terror, Wamba took part in a raid on a mission outpost. The missionary, an elderly man from Scotland, was put to death with typical Mau-Mau hideousness. But instead of feeling the satisfaction he believed the death of any enemy should give him, Wamba returned home strangely shaken. He lay down in his mud-and-wattle house, but he could not sleep. He could not forget the dying man's face. There was no fear, no self-pity and, most astonishing of all, no hate. The old man seemed completely at peace. What kind of religion was this, Wamba asked himself, that gave a man this kind of victory?

Not long afterward, Wamba was arrested by government troops and, with thousands of other suspected Mau Mau, herded into a detention camp. There, something peculiar began to happen. Night after night, instead of joining the talk of escape and revenge, Wamba found himself remembering the missionary's face. There in prison he began to wonder for the first time whether hatred and violence really were the answer for his people.

One day a group of young African Christians came to the prison to hold services. They were Kikuyu from a village near Wamba's. Wamba knew that one of them had had a brother killed by the Mau Mau, another a wife. Yet instead of railing against those who had committed these crimes, the young men spoke of forgiveness, reconciliation, love.

"We're not going to say that you should love," they continued, "without telling you how this happened for us. Love is the result of an experience. It is the miracle that takes place when the Spirit of Jesus comes into your life."

Wamba found himself listening with an excitement that astonished him. Day after day as the young men came back to preach, he felt a growing desire to have this miracle for himself. At last one day he rose to his feet, and while his fellow prisoners stared in disbelief—hardly believing it himself—he said: "I would like this Spirit to come to me. What do I do?"

After the meeting the young evangelists prayed with Wamba. It wasn't then, however, but that night as he lay alone on his mat in the night barracks, that the miracle occurred. Wamba felt an indescribable lightness, as though the weight of rage that had pressed down on him for so many years had been lifted from him. He knew for sure now that Christ was real; in place of the rage was an overwhelming compassion.

From the moment of that first question in the prison compound, Wamba was a scorned outcast among the freedom fighters of Kenya. His farm was burned, his cattle cut with *panga* knives, his wife and children afraid to leave their *shamba*. But not only did he refuse to deny that he was a Christian; by the time of his release the conviction had grown in him that he must become a minister of this new way of love.

We grasped a little of the enormity of this idea from our experience at St. Paul's. Not only for Wamba, but for most Africans, entering the ministry means embracing a life of perpetual poverty. Until such local theological schools as St. Paul's were established, clergymen appeared mysteriously from abroad, supported by congregations in some distant and unimaginable place. The concept of a local congregation having responsibility for its clergy is new to much of Africa. Few of these college students would know the privilege of full-time ministry; most would continue to farm or find factory work to support themselves.

But Wamba was sure of his call. One Sunday we went with him to the church in Ngecha where he'd already begun serving. Wamba had referred to it as a small church, but even from a distance we could see it towering above the countryside; a young cathedral in stone, with towering gables and immense Gothic windows.

As we drove closer, however, we saw that the impressive silhouette was only a skeleton; the arched windows had no glass, the building had neither floor nor roof. It was a relic of the days when European culture was imported along with the Christian faith; when steep-roofed Gothic churches were erected in lands where it never snows, because "that's how churches look." Begun before the Mau-Mau terror in Kenya had slowed donations from British missions, the church had not so much a half-finished look as a half-abandoned one.

The congregation was arriving. Old men leaning on sticks, women with babies at their breasts, little girls with the next-to-youngest child on their backs. Each person there faced what Wamba faced; the knowledge that his neighbors despised him for his beliefs. Yet here they were.

The song leader stepped up to the big drum beside the pulpit and beat out the rhythm of the opening hymn. Prayers in Kikuyu followed. A sermon. More singing. Sitting on a wooden plank with the sky as our ceiling, we witnessed an enthusiasm and a discipline and a depth of fellowship such as we'd rarely experienced in America and Europe.

At the end of the service, the collection was taken. We glanced into the grass basket when it reached our row. There were six penny coppers in it, two eggs, and an ear of corn. We sang a last hymn to the beat of the drum, and after farewell embraces all around, we drove away.

Wamba was staying on for a second service later in the day. We've never forgotten our last glimpse of that church, standing roofless in a hostile countryside, and Wamba cradling two speckled eggs tenderly in one hand while with the other he waved good-bye.

This man and this church typify, we believe, both the problems and the strengths of Christians in emerging nations. Problems are many. Christianity is associated everywhere with the colonialism so recently thrown off. To be a Christian is to be hated, persecuted, possibly killed.

But the strengths are more impressive still. The essential requirement for a growing church has never been safety. The requirement is the ability to respond to hatred with love—and this Wamba and each member of his congregation has been enabled to do. "Love your enemies," Jesus commanded. "Bless them that curse you, do good to them that hate you." All over the Third World today, Christians are showing us how.

John and Elizabeth

The Child Nobody Wanted

Love can't be defined. It can only be experienced.

Peter was not a "lovable" child. Since his parents had died, he'd been shuttled from one family to another, not wanted, not belonging. Now, at the age of five, he was protecting himself from a world that didn't want him by rejecting that world. Peter wouldn't talk; he wouldn't smile; he hated everybody.

At the Hillcrest Adoption Service, they'd just about given up finding a home for Peter. My friend Isobel Clarke is a case worker there and often talked to me about Peter. "It would take a miracle to make that boy risk loving someone again," she said.

And then one day Mrs. Greene came to the Service. Mrs. Greene told Isobel that she and her husband had waited fifteen years for a child of their own; now they knew there wouldn't be one. Isobel hardly heard her; she was staring at Mrs. Greene, thinking she had never seen a face so full of love. And as she looked at her, Isobel was thinking, *Peter*.

She told Mrs. Greene about him and saw her eyes shine at the idea of having a little boy of her own. "But I'm frightened," Isobel admitted to me. "Peter is such a badly hurt little boy. Mrs. Greene won't believe me when I tell her that he hates everybody. She hasn't seen him yet."

It was a long time before Mrs. Greene could see Peter. First there had to be interviews, medical reports, family histories—the Adoption Service puts prospective parents and child together with infinite pains before they are ever allowed to meet.

But at last the great day came when Mrs. Greene was to see Peter for the first time. Peter was taken to the park to play on the swings. Mrs. Greene and Isobel were to sit down on one of the benches where Mrs. Greene could watch him without his knowing that he was being "considered."

As Isobel walked with Mrs. Greene to the park, her heart was pounding so hard she was afraid Mrs. Greene would hear it. She knew, as she'd never known anything before, that this woman and this little boy belonged together. *But, dear God, let them know it too,* she prayed as they neared the gate. *Don't let her see just his tense, angry little face! Don't let this first meeting be so bad it spoils the rest!*

For there would be other meetings of course: another "chance" meeting—next time with Mr. Greene as well—then a visit to Peter's current foster home, then . . . But so much depended on this first time!

They were through the gate now, and Isobel saw Peter a little way off, near the swings. He wasn't swinging, he was standing next to the fence, his eyes on the ground.

Isobel turned to Mrs. Greene with an encouraging smile, but she seemed to have forgotten Isobel was there. Her eyes were fixed on Peter.

The next moment Mrs. Greene was walking straight toward him. *No, no!* thought Isobel, hurrying after her. This was all wrong! Peter must never guess that they were watching him. Mrs. Greene was almost running now. Peter looked up and saw her, and he too started running—not away, but toward her.

Now they stopped, a foot apart, neither of them speaking, just looking at each other. Isobel caught up with them.

"Peter," she said, "do you know who this lady is?"

"Yes," said Peter. His eyes never left Mrs. Greene's face as he answered. "She's my mother."

Elizabeth

Helene's Story: Part One

She grew up in a world of hate. Could she believe in a God of love?

In Austria in 1989, John and I met an exceptional woman. We'd been attending a weekly Bible study in a neighbor's living room, with its painted wooden furniture and immense green-tiled heating stove. One evening, however, an unusual sight met us as we pulled off boots and mittens just inside the door. On the table sat not the customary coffee and strudel, but . . . matzo . . . a lamb bone . . . a bundle of leeks. . . .

On the far side of the table sat a white-bearded man in a fringed prayer shawl. When the rest of us had taken seats, he began to speak—in American-accented English—relating this Passover Seder to the Last Supper of Jesus.

At his side an Austrian woman, nearer sixty than fifty, translated his talk into German. Afterwards, over coffee and pastry (which had been waiting in the kitchen), John and I introduced ourselves to the speaker as fellow Americans. He told us he was the son, grandson, and great-grandson of rabbis, most of whose family had perished here under the Nazis. It was to prevent future tragedies like the Holocaust that he and Helene, his translator, were doing these teaching programs.

I looked around at the clusters of young men and women, discussing what was clearly their first exposure to the Jewish faith. In the entire room only the four of us were old enough to remember the Nazi era.

"You were here then, in 1938," I said to Helene, "when Hitler marched into Salzburg."

"I saw it!" She and her mother, she said, had taken a train to the city to join the thousands cheering Hitler's motorcade. "That's why I believe so in what we're doing tonight." Germany, she said, had in some measure faced up to its history. "Not Austria. Here we still like to believe we were victims of the Nazis, not partners."

"We all do that," I said. "Nations, individuals—we all try to gloss over the mistakes of the past."

"But if we don't bring our past to God, all of it," said Helene, "how can he heal us? I was a Nazi, you see. I believed in Hitler with all my heart. How could I have made a new beginning if I denied that?"

John and I exchanged looks of astonishment. For over forty years, in repeated visits in both Germany and Austria, we had never before met a person who'd admit to being a former Nazi. We had so many questions that we canceled the rest of our travel plans to remain in Austria. How had it been possible for millions of ordinary, decent people to be deceived by Hitler? Here is Helene's story.

The groundwork for the Nazi horror was laid, Helene said, with the collapse of Austria's economy after the First World War. Born in 1930, the youngest of four children, Helene couldn't remember when her family had been the sole occupants of the house in Puch, nine miles from Salzburg. By the 1930s the six Obermayers lived in a few rooms on the second floor, while the local police department occupied the ground floor. Helene's first memory was of beggars at the door. At least Helene's parents, both schoolteachers, had jobs at a time when a quarter of the population was out of work.

Then, when Helene was four, a car, taking the twisting mountain roads too fast, struck her father as he pedaled his bicycle home from school. Helene's father was a mountain climber. With his tremendous heart and lungs, it took him four weeks to die.

Her mother's salary barely put food on the table. The eldest child, Thusnelda, took a job in a shop, but rising prices gobbled up the few shillings she earned. Hermann, the next oldest, left school in 1934, a few months after his father's death. Like most young Austrian men, however, Hermann could find no work at all.

Meanwhile, just over the border in Germany, the economy was booming through the efforts of a leader named Adolf Hitler. For decades thoughtful people had been saying that the two German-speaking nations should be united. Why not now under this energetic man who was an Austrian himself?

The Austrian government, fearing overthrow, outlawed Hitler's Nazi party, but many Austrians, including Hermann, joined in secret. One night in 1936 Hermann had news.

Six-year-old Helene had gotten a fire going in the old wood-burning stove so that her mother could put on their meal of cabbage and potatoes when she got home from school. Hermann could hardly wait until the plates were served. One of his friends had been to Berchtesgaden, only a few miles away in Germany. "There are jobs there, Mama! And they pay in good German marks!"

"But the border guard?" his mother objected. Austrian troops patrolled the frontier.

Hermann shrugged. "I'll go over the mountain."

Helene nodded. Most mealtime conversation was over

her head, but she did know about mountains. Before her father died, the family spent each weekend climbing. Her happiest memories were of sitting astride a pair of broad shoulders high above the clouds.

Enthusiastically Hermann described the "Eagle's Nest" Hitler was building above Berchtesgaden. Hitler . . . that was another memory of her adored father—how he would stand a little taller when he spoke of this new leader of the German-speaking people. "Hard work and self-discipline," he would quote the Führer, "will make us great again."

From then on the family saw Hermann only occasionally, always at night, and always bringing money. The police on the first floor of the building soon noticed his absence—and the fact that Mrs. Obermayer occasionally stopped now at the butcher's shop. "Where is he?" they kept asking. "The moment he returns, he must report to us."

In 1937 Thusnelda set her wedding date. Her fiancé was a well-known violinist, and the family was delighted—except for fears concerning Hermann. Though the younger boy, Helmut, was now fifteen, Hermann would regard it his solemn duty as the elder son to take his father's place at the ceremony.

But the police, of course, knew this too.

An hour before the wedding Hermann slipped through the back door. The police were waiting for him. They arrested not only him, but Helmut too, on suspicion that they were members of the illegal Nazi party. Mrs. Obermayer went downstairs to plead with the police. "Let the boys come with us to church. I give you my word they will return here."

So Hermann led Thusnelda down the aisle. Afterwards, true to their mother's promise, Hermann and Helmut reported to the police. Upstairs, guests had assembled for the reception. Helene was passing a tray of cakes when the beatings began. From the room below came a thud, then a scream. Another blow, another scream. The wedding party stood in frozen groups, no one speaking. The sickening sounds went on all afternoon.

Late that night the boys were released, bruised and bleeding, but triumphant. The rubber hoses had not drawn from them a single name of their Nazi comrades.

The next day, Helene dipped the tail of her black-and-white terrier in a can of red paint, making him, too, a hero in the Nazis' red, white, and black. From its hiding place among her hair ribbons, she took out Hitler's picture and dreamed that, like her brothers, she would have a chance to suffer for him.

Then in March 1938 the Nazis marched into Austria. Her mother took Helene into Salzburg so that the eight-year-old could someday describe the great moment to her children. With thousands of others they stood on the Schwarzstrasse, waving small red paper flags bearing the black swastika in a white circle. As the motorcade drove slowly past the Mozarteum, Helene shouted herself hoarse. But when last of all, in a long open car, came Hitler himself, she was too overcome with adoration to make a sound.

As the Führer had promised, there was soon work for all. Hitler's enemies attacked—he said that would happen too—and Hermann and Helmut rushed to join the army. Helene had to wait till she was ten to don the black skirt and brown jacket of the Hitler Youth, her long blonde plaits swinging as she marched.

It was at these youth meetings that Helene heard the Nazi explanation of Austria's past misery; all was due to "the wickedness of Jews." To Helene especially, this seemed plausible. Hadn't it been a Jew driving the car that killed her father? Rage blazed inside her as the leader explained that

Jews were rich because they were thieves. That was why her father had had only a bicycle to ride, while Jews could go speeding about in cars.

Hatred for these people grew as strong as her love for Hitler. Helene was not sure she'd ever actually seen a Jew, but she knew from the Hitler Youth posters what they looked like: they were fat, with greedy eyes, enormous noses, and thick fingers covered with rings. She cried with relief when told that Hitler would not allow these evil men to hurt her anymore.

Girls in the Hitler Youth kept busy knitting socks and mittens for the soldiers at the front. Then in 1943 the first bombing raids struck Salzburg, and Helene's squadron was trained in rescue work. Salzburg's ancient cathedral was gutted; the house where Mozart grew up was destroyed. Digging in the rubble for survivors after each raid, Helene developed a new hatred.

Americans.

It was their planes that were killing helpless people, destroying all that was beautiful. Austria was winning the war, of course; Hitler said so. It was frustration that made the Americans so destructive.

The raids only increased Helene's commitment. She was attending secondary school in Salzburg now. When the train tracks were bombed, she proudly walked the nine miles each way.

In 1945, with American land forces drawing near, Helene was trained to handle a bazooka. To her squadron of teenage girls would fall the honor of helping to defend Berchtesgaden against the approaching tanks. Helene was eager to die protecting the Führer. It was from his Eagle's Nest that Hitler would unleash his secret weapon that would send the Americans fleeing back across the ocean.

And then . . . suddenly American soldiers were in Salzburg. Like other Austrian women, Helene, her mother, and her sister, with Thusnelda's small children, fled to the mountains. For five months they hid out, living in a hut they'd built for mountain climbing holidays, foraging in the fields for food.

But at last cold weather forced them back to Puch. The occupying American troops did not appear to be the atrocity-prone barbarians the women had been led to expect. Still, no decent Austrian girl would dream of returning their glances.

Thus for Helene the bleak postwar years began. Hermann and Helmut returned home disabled; all of her cousins, twelve young men, had died at the front. Thusnelda's husband, the violinist, came back shattered by years in a Russian prison camp. Their daughter, Helene's little niece, died of typhus that winter.

Along with these losses went another, invisible but just as real—betrayal by the man Helene had worshiped as a savior.

In his speeches Hitler had assured the Austrians right up to the final days that they were winning the war. Now it was clear that he had lied. But . . . could a savior lie?

Helene moved through her late teens in a fog of bewilderment. After leaving school she trained as a dental technician and got a job at an American military hospital. And here Helene had her second crippling shock. Hitler had lied about the war. Now at the hospital she encountered another lie. Several of the American Army dentists were Jews, the first she had ever met face to face. But . . . they were not fat, they wore no rings. They looked and acted, in fact, exactly like everyone else.

These shell holes in a mind and heart once filled with certainties might not show on the outside, but year by year the inner emptiness grew. Helene struggled to fill it in all kinds of ways: in business success as she turned to marketing dental supplies, in music, in skating, and skiing.

Above all, in mountain climbing. Here alone, for a few hours, she could believe that life had meaning. On these rocky heights she could feel herself in contact with something . . . nonmaterial. Helene's family had not been churchgoers, but the Presence she felt on the mountaintops was somehow spiritual. Transcendent. And yet . . . tender too, intimate, caring, like the love she'd felt from her father, long ago, on these same peaks.

She couldn't maintain it, this strange communion of the heights. She would descend into the valley—into the shame and horror that for twenty-five years had made up her inner life. For Helene had seen photographs of the Nazi extermination camps. Many of her countrymen refused to believe they were genuine. Helene's brother-in-law explained to her that the camps had been created as propaganda by the occupation forces. Though it meant the end of his career as a violinist, he refused to renounce his Nazi ties. He died in 1979 believing to the end that the murder of 6 million innocent men, women, and children had never happened.

But it had happened. Hideous as the truth was, Helene preferred it to the lies she had been raised on. Truth, it seemed to her, however hard, must be the thing that at last she could truly trust.

Then in 1974 Helene attended a business seminar in Germany, where one of the speakers exuded the kind of certainty she longed for. Lingering afterwards, she told him of her own quest for truth. "Jesus is the truth," the man replied. What is more, he went on, the truth was that Jesus loved her.

Wistfully Helene heard him describe this love of Jesus as a free, unmerited gift. "We can do nothing to earn it." That, certainly, was true. No amount of success had freed her from the self-hatred that had blighted all her adult life.

"But is he real, this Jesus?" she asked. Once before she'd put her faith in a savior. "I have to know if he is real."

The man smiled. "Ask him," he said.

And so she did, that night, alone in her room. "Jesus," she said, "I never again want to believe what is not true. If you *are* real, please show me."

She recognized him at once. He was with her in the room—with her, within her, all around her—the Presence she had known so often on the mountaintop. So real that the rest of her life till that moment seemed only make-believe. So real she knew he would not let her go until his love had made her whole.

Elizabeth

Helene's Story: Part Two

God loved her. But would a man ever love her too?

Smiling at her own foolishness, Helene Obermayer drew out a sheet of paper and wrote across the top:

MY IDEAL HUSBAND
He should have beautiful hands.
He should love classical music.
He should sometimes let me drive the car.

Helene looked at the third line and almost scratched it out. Most Austrian women, even in 1975, did not drive. Certainly a married woman wouldn't need to. But Helene loved driving. As sales representative for a dental supply company, she felt her hours behind the wheel with her cocker spaniel at her side were the best in any week.

The next moment she scrunched up the paper and tossed it on the floor. How ridiculous for a forty-five-year-old spinster to sit daydreaming about marriage like a romantic teenager!

Her own teenage years had been spent in the shadow of the Second World War, first as a member of a Hitler Youth squadron that mobilized young girls to defend their homeland, then in the bitter postwar years of the American occupation.

To Helene, the hunger, the cold, the bomb damage had been nothing compared with the discovery that the leader she had worshiped, Adolf Hitler, was in fact a bloodthirsty tyrant. Her disillusionment was so enormous that for thirty years she let herself trust no one—certainly not the kind of trust that could lead to marriage.

Then twelve months earlier, in 1974, Helene had learned that God loved her. Daring to trust his love, she had begun, slowly, shyly, over the past year to wonder if someday she could know a man's love, too.

"Ridiculous!" Helene repeated. She scooped the sheet of paper from the floor and threw it into a wastepaper basket. Where would she meet an unattached man at all, let alone one with a certain sort of hands and musical taste? There were pitifully few Austrian men her age or older; virtually that whole generation had died in Hitler's armies, and those who survived had long since married.

But as the months passed, the desire for a husband only grew stronger. A year after writing out that childish list, she was praying one day, when into her mind, as clear as a photograph in her hand, came the vision of a man. *This is the husband,* she thought she heard God say, *whom I am giving you.*

Helene's mouth went dry; her heart pounded. In speechless astonishment she considered the picture in her mind. The man had intense dark eyes, beetling black eyebrows, a full head of wavy white hair. The "picture," in black and white, was of his head and shoulders only. But what she could see of his clothes told her something more: a jacket in a hideous pattern of crisscross stripes, and the ugliest tie Helene had ever seen.

He was an American. She was as sure of it as she was that God himself was showing him to her. But Americans had been the enemy! The invaders. Was it possible that God was asking her to love a man from the country she'd hated with all her heart?

Or was this always God's answer? Where we've hated most, to plant the deepest love?

At any rate, Helene began to pray daily for this person she had "seen," and to look for him everywhere she went—sales conventions, church retreats, concert halls. But 1977 came and went, then 1978. Though the portrait in her mind remained as sharp as ever, no such individual appeared.

Three full years passed; Helene decided she must have mistaken her own longing for the voice of God.

Meanwhile, reading the Bible each day, she was eager to visit the Holy Land. In 1979 she joined a church group on a tour of Israel.

And it was there, in the conference hall of a hotel on the Golan Heights, that she saw him. He was wearing a short-sleeved shirt in place of the awful jacket and tie she had seen in her vision. But the intent eyes, the heavy brows, the white hair—she would have recognized him anywhere.

And now what? Could she walk up to a total stranger and say, "You're supposed to be my husband"?

Heart in her mouth, Helene worked her way toward the man across the crowded lobby. "Excuse me," she said, feeling a flush burn her cheeks, "I think—it seems to me I've seen you somewhere."

So they exchanged introductions. Gideon Miller, as Helene had guessed, was an American. She invented excuses to keep chatting, long enough to learn that he was presently managing a small bookshop in Jerusalem. How did he like living in Israel? Very much. "For us Jews, you know, it's a lifelong dream."

Us Jews. For a searing moment Helene saw herself in the black-and-brown uniform of the Hitler Youth, swallowing the poison of anti-Semitism. *Was* God going to leave no rag of prejudice unwashed in his love? Had he really chosen as her husband not only an American, but a Jew?

When her tour group got to Jerusalem she located the shop where Gideon worked. A tape recorder was playing as she stepped in, a Chopin sonata. "My weakness," Gideon confessed. "I'll go without lunch to buy music."

Startled, Helene recalled the "ideal husband" she'd daydreamed about four years before. A music lover . . . with beautiful hands . . . who would let her drive the car. She looked at Gideon's hands. Slender and strong, with long, tapering fingers.

As they talked, Helene learned that Gideon, like herself, had carried a burden of rage. For him the fury was against Germans—and Austrians in particular—who had murdered all but a handful of his family. Coming from opposite sides of a tragic history, the souls of this middle-aged man and woman groped toward each other there in that dusty book-shop in Jerusalem.

Suddenly Gideon turned and began rummaging in a drawer. "I don't know why I'm doing this," Helene heard him mutter.

He straightened up. "I've never in my life given anyone a picture of myself," he said, clearly baffled at his own behav-ior, "but . . ." He thrust a photograph at her. "This was taken three years ago."

Helene held it in her hands, as she'd held it so long in her heart. The photograph of a white-haired man with com-pelling eyes . . . the striped jacket . . . the terrible tie.

With this evidence of God's purpose in her hands, Helene waited expectantly for him to reveal the design to Gideon as well. All that week in Jerusalem she dreamed up devices to throw the two of them together, asking him to show her numerous landmarks, spending hours on her hair and makeup.

But Gideon, though cordial enough, seemed to regard Helene as nothing more than an especially determined sightseer. Eight years older than she, he had had an unhappy marriage in his youth, and after the death of his wife remained a bachelor. Marriage was obviously the last thing on his mind.

And there was an added impediment, Helene realized, as her tour group boarded the plane for home. Gideon was struggling with prejudice as Helene had. But his root of bitterness went deeper—based not on lies but on the terrible reality of the Holocaust.

From Austria Helene began writing to Gideon, describing the centuries-old isolation of Jews that had made possible the Nazi hate campaign, urging him to visit Austria as a teacher and a bridge builder. Such teaching, she told him honestly enough, was desperately needed. What she couldn't mention was her personal motive.

For months Gideon resisted the suggestion. But he was above all a praying man. At last he wrote that God was directing him to come.

Helene met him at Salzburg Airport. Before getting into the car she handed him the keys. He stared at them in dismay. "I'm sorry, Helene. Would you mind terribly? You see, I've never learned to drive."

Joyfully Helene chauffeured him about the country, translating for him as he preached. As invitations multiplied, he returned to Austria again, then a third time. And still, for all Helene could see, she remained simply his driver and interpreter. Occasionally she would find him staring at her with a look so tortured, so intense she would turn away in confusion. But about his feelings he never spoke.

The night before Helene's fiftieth birthday was the lowest point of all. Gideon had spoken that evening in Wuppertal, Germany. "There's nothing scheduled for tomorrow," he said as she dropped him at the private home where he was to spend the night. "So we won't need to get together."

". . . won't *need* . . . I won't *need* you . . ." All the way to the women's hostel where Helene was staying on the other side of town, the crushing word pursued her. It was need alone that made him seek her out.

She cried herself to sleep and awoke to a dismal birthday in a strange city. In Salzburg friends had planned a great celebration on this fiftieth milestone. Instead she was alone, far from home, chasing a dream of marriage to a man who tolerated her presence only as a practicality.

She wandered disconsolately into a small bookshop, looking for something to read. There was a rack near the entrance, and in it . . . a solitary birthday card.

Why, those were Alpine flowers decorating it! The very ones Helene had picked as a child on the mountains above Salzburg. Suddenly Helene knew that this was *her* card, her special birthday greeting from God. With trembling fingers she opened it to the message:

> Blessings on your Birthday
> What God has promised, that will He also do
> (Romans 4:21)

That birthday card kept Helene from despairing as still another year passed, then eighteen months. Gideon was spending more and more time in Austria, depending on her German translations at his meetings—but nothing more.

The card reassured her when she discovered a lump in her breast. God had promised her a husband, *this* husband, so how could she die before he brought it about?

In the spring of 1982 she was told she must have an

operation. The day before the surgery Gideon came up to the hospital room with a letter postponing their speaking dates until Helene was well enough to travel again. At a table in the room she shared with three other patients, Helene was translating his English draft into German when Gideon suddenly laid his hand over the page.

"Helene . . . will you come outside with me?"

Startled, Helene looked out of the window. It was pouring rain. Something in Gideon's eyes, though, stifled her objections—the look of anguish she had caught there before. She dressed swiftly and followed him down the stairs and into the garden behind the hospital. The rain had driven everyone else inside, creating the only private spot in that busy place. Walking close together beneath his black umbrella, they'd gone halfway down the path when Gideon stopped.

"Helene, will you marry me?"

He had fallen in love with her, he rushed on to say, that very first week in Jerusalem—and struggled against it every day for the past three years. "I gave myself all the logical reasons why we could never be close. But, Helene . . . dear one, it's almost as though our being together had all been planned ahead of time."

"A long, long time ahead," said Helene.

Surgery revealed a benign tumor. Gideon and Helene were married in the autumn of that year. Today they lead groups of Austrians on missions of repentance to the sites of local concentration camps. They've come a long way, the former Nazi and the Jew.

Elizabeth

The Mechanical Man

They called the great golfer the "Texas Iceberg"—not only because of his coldly machine-like play, but because he froze out the fans.

"Since I was knee-high to a grasshopper," Ben Hogan told us, "I've had to fight for everything I got." His introduction to the game of golf was a case in point.

The son of a blacksmith, twelve-year-old Hogan was selling newspapers at Union Station in Fort Worth, Texas, when he heard that caddies at a golf club outside town were making sixty-five cents a round. He went after the job without the slightest idea what golf was.

The caddy boss sized Hogan up, picked out another youngster who wanted to work, and told them to box each other for the job. The winner would be taken on. Ben won.

After a year of caddying he decided to try the game himself. Hogan didn't have a natural swing. But he understood work and attention to detail. One of his own caddies commented years later, "He'll memorize the grain of the grass if it will help his game." Hogan, the golfing machine, was born.

It was a plodding, mechanical, intellectual approach to the game that brought Hogan to the foremost rank of players. "He swings with the businesslike authority of a machine stamping out bottle tops," one reporter wrote. Hogan himself, describing his swing, used the tip-off phrase, "muscle memory."

To memorize a stroke muscle by muscle takes hours of solitary practice. Although this isolated concentration paid off in Ben's game, it took its toll on his personality. Hogan became dour, taciturn. On the links he did not know how to handle the distraction of the audience—the hero worship, jibes, requests for autographs. The solution he found was to shut himself off from the crowd.

These are not qualities to make a popular man, but they did make a champion. By 1945 Ben was winning title after title. En masse, the audiences did not like him. But there was something about the very shyness and metallic discipline of this small man of just over 125 pounds that doubtless made many of the silent watchers decide, "I'm probably the only one here who does, but I like that guy Hogan."

Then, tragedy. On the morning of February 2, 1949, Hogan was critically injured in a car accident. The golf champion had a crushed pelvis, a fractured left leg, a crushed shoulder, and a broken ankle. Doctors hoped he would live, but doubted if he would ever walk again. Nobody even considered the possibility that Ben Hogan would resume his golf career.

It wasn't much more than a year later that Hogan amazed the world by entering the Los Angeles Open—one of the top tournaments in the country. Although in agony with leg cramps, Ben limped to the first tee as the crowd cheered. Instead of the tense, fixed expression usually reserved for the audience, Hogan's face broke into a warm smile.

Ben played his usual concentrated game. His courage and determination brought him a tie in the seventy-two hole match. He lost the playoff, but everyone was speaking of "Hogan's victory."

The performance was remarkable in itself, but the change in the "Texas Iceberg" was even more so. Hogan went on to win the U.S. Open, and in 1951 the Master's—and he went on acknowledging the cheers of the audience. When we visited him in Hershey, we asked what accounted for both his physical and his psychological healing.

On the physical side, he said, he relied on his technique of muscle memory: if he practiced a given golf shot long enough and with enough concentration, his muscles would learn the movements until they became almost automatic. On his hospital bed he applied the same theory. If he concentrated hard enough on rehabilitating his crippled limbs one function at a time—if he believed enough and put that belief into practice during endless hours of therapy—then just as he'd mastered golf he could remaster control of his body.

And the belief? Where did that kind of conviction come from?

"From the letters." By the thousands they'd poured into that hospital room. Letters from all kinds of people: housewives, salesmen, office workers, students, bus drivers, bankers—each with basically the same message: "You can make it, Ben. We're praying for you."

"I was stunned. Nothing of this sort had ever happened to me. I'd grown up believing you fight for what you want, seeing people only as competitors. On the golf course I'd tried to shut myself off from spectators so that I could concentrate on my game. Before these letters came, I told myself that I never cared much whether people were for me or against me."

All this changed with that outpouring of love and prayer through the mail. "The prayers of people I never knew—and those of my wife, Valerie—are the reason for my recovery. Their belief in me helped me believe in myself. I had to repay faith with faith."

The three of us talked for over two leisurely hours. There was nothing cold or ungiving about this great athlete. He spoke eloquently of the people who had helped him, his wife's tireless patience—and of his friends in the audience.

Early in his life Ben Hogan found the strength of determination and discipline. Through the caring of others he discovered the strength of love.

John and Elizabeth

Learning to Forgive Others

Seeing God as love.

Meeting the people whose stories we've just told, it hasn't been hard for John and me to see God as love . . . for them. What's sometimes been harder has been to believe that this love extends to ourselves. We've made a discovery, though. When God seems uncaring, the blockage is always on our part, usually in some human relationship broken and festering. There's a God-given way to heal this brokenness.

In Herman Melville's classic, *Moby Dick,* Captain Ahab, maimed by a vicious white whale, spends the rest of his life attempting to rid the seas of this menace. But in his seemingly admirable intent to destroy evil, he himself becomes evil; the battle costs him his soul as well as his life.

Captain Ahab's tragedy points to a universal truth: Harm done to us, any harm, can in the end utterly destroy us unless we master the lesson Captain Ahab never learned—how to forgive.

1. Discover where hurt still rankles

Is it a good idea to dredge up old wounds and bruises? Not if we stop there. Simply to uncover buried resentment would do no more good than for a dentist to uncover decay in a tooth and leave it alone. In order to clean out the decay, however, the dentist must first pick and probe—even at the cost of temporary pain. Before we can clear away old areas of unforgiveness, we must first locate them.

We've found that a small notebook helps here. Each time the smart of a betrayal or injury assails you, summarize it in a few words in your notebook and turn the page. Later, you'll be using these notes in a creative way.

To speed up the process, here are five headings which can serve as a jog to memory. Ask God to bring these painful recollections to your conscious mind, where you and he can deal with them. A long-submerged grudge may rise to the surface when you least expect it, so keep your notebook handy!

Time—A difficult period in your life: your teens, early married years, a particular job.

Place—The location where a painful experience took place: on a trip, at a party, in a classroom.

Person—"Problem" personalities: a neighbor, teacher, parent, sister, boss.

Circumstance—A confidence betrayed, a deceit, a theft.

Emotion—When did you feel humiliated, cheated, outraged, helpless?

Jot one-line descriptions of these occasions in your notebook. These are the semiforgotten but far from disposed-of areas of ill will that you have had to live with, perhaps for many years. If there are a lot of them, your memory is serving you well—injuries are common in an imperfect world. If there are just a few, you are a good forgiver. Or, you may be especially adept at covering up negative feelings, in which case you may have to stick with this "dental checkup" stage longer.

2. Apply your intellect

The first step toward healing is understanding. Consider, for instance, the bully who beat you up, or the coach who ridiculed you, or the office manager who corrected you in front of the staff. From the vantage point of time, can you form any idea why they acted as they did? All action has meaning. What was the message of these attacks upon you? Was the bully really afraid? The office manager jealous?

The more serious the injury—from an abusive parent, an alcoholic spouse, a mugger—the more certain we can be that the injuring individual has himself suffered some profound trauma. Where it is possible to know the background, outrage is often tempered by compassion.

3. Hold your attacker up to God

So far you have identified areas of hurt and you have tried to understand the person who harmed you. The next step is deliberately to lift that person into God's healing light. Remember that God continues to love him no matter what his offense. Think of him as bathed in this love; see him as being given the strength and satisfaction he so badly needs. Intercede on his behalf before God, bringing as many specifics into your prayer as you can.

This is a key step. You are here *acting* forgiveness, whether you feel it yet or not, by seeking the welfare of your enemy. He has hurt you out of weakness. You know from experience how much pain this failing in him can cause. You can certainly pray for this weakness to be healed before damage is done in still more lives.

4. Let the Holy Spirit intercede

Helpful as understanding and intercession are, there is a limit to the insight and initiative we can bring to our own hurts. We are seeing things from the viewpoint of the wronged party and our very human reactions get in the way. It is here that the Holy Spirit comes to our aid.

"The Spirit also helpeth our infirmities," wrote Paul. "For we know not what we should pray for as we ought: but the Spirit itself maketh intercession for us with groanings which cannot be uttered" (Romans 8:26).

Work as hard as possible to understand and pray for your debtor, then relax and ask the Holy Spirit to complete the job for you. This experience may or may not be accompanied by a feeling of warmth for the person you are releasing. It doesn't matter. This is an act of faith, not of emotion. "I ask you, Holy Spirit, to do what I am unable to do. Help me release [name] to you for all the blessings you have in store for him."

5. Demonstrate change of heart

Wherever practical, find a way to show your former antagonist that the wound is healed. Be subtle: a too sudden or too direct approach can backfire. If you are rejected in your efforts, don't worry. Just continue to hold him up to God.

As a final gesture of having put the hurt behind you, rip out that page from your notebook and put a match to it. We find it helpful to think of the smoke as prayer, lifting this event into God's all-seeing, all-healing presence.

6. Practice daily forgiveness

A wonderful new awareness of God's love for you will follow the laying-down of these ancient burdens of resentment. But since we live in a sinful world, we can be sure that in days to come, new treacheries, new hurts will again blur our vision of him. We need to learn to make forgiveness spontaneous and habitual.

An ancient rule is never to let the sun go down on our wrath. Certainly we should never go to sleep without first passing the day in review, lifting any hurtful episode to God for healing. If we do this faithfully, then bitterness and grudge-bearing will never again have a chance to set up their destructive patterns in our lives.

Elizabeth

Learning to Forgive Ourselves

Suppose, though, that the person you've refused to forgive is not someone else, but yourself. It's a strange fact that many of us find it easier to forgive others than to believe that we ourselves are forgiven. Why should this be so hard? The answer may lie in one of the following areas. How could you answer these questions:

Do I really believe in a forgiving God? Don't be too quick to answer yes. Many of our deepest feelings about God were formed in childhood. Punishment, a wrathful father, the consequences of our own misbehavior—all of these early impressions probably play a larger role in our real image of God than phrases we learn later about his mercy.

Do I believe that when God forgives my sins he also forgets them? Certainly we don't forget our own wrong thoughts and actions; psychiatrists' offices are crowded with people reliving ancient errors. Neither does society forget: one transgression against the law can brand a person for life. Do you believe God's promises when he says, "I will forgive their iniquity, and I will remember their sin no more" (Jeremiah 31:34)?

Does it seem to me that my sin is too shameful to be forgiven? The Bible speaks of only one unforgivable sin: blasphemy against the Holy Spirit. No other transgression is beyond God's willingness to forgive and to forget.

Have I fulfilled the prerequisite to forgiveness? Have I forgiven any who have injured me? "If ye forgive not men their trespasses," Jesus cautions, "neither will your Father forgive your trespasses" (Matthew 6:15). That is why learning to forgive others is the first phase in restoring our vision of God.

Getting started

Let's assume we're ready to make an in-depth experiment in accepting God's forgiveness. For the purposes of the experiment, choose a situation, perhaps of long standing, about which you feel guilty.

Step one: Be specific. In an effort to get away from uncomfortable feelings, we sometimes camouflage our guilt in generalities. Perhaps, for example, you are feeling vaguely guilty over the bombing of Hiroshima. As citizens we share of course in social guilt, but the roots of these large tragedies are hatred and indifference on the part of individuals. What "seeds of war" in your own heart need God's forgiveness? Perhaps it's a coworker or a neighbor against whom you harbor ill will.

It's also tempting to focus guilt on a bad habit rather than on the cause of the habit. Maybe you berate yourself for drinking too much, when behind the drinking is the more serious sin of self-hatred. Stop the destructive behavior of course! But at the same time come to grips with the deeper evil.

Try always to work your way back from the many to the one, the abstract to the specific, the effect to the cause. The recognition of our own particular and personal shortcomings is the first step to obtaining forgiveness.

Step two: Repent. There are many different ways of regretting a mistake, some of which get us off the track that leads to true forgiveness. Which of these describes your present mood?

• Wounded pride. This kind of remorse begins with the thought, *How could I have done that?* It is ego-centered.

• Fence-straddling. I feel regret, yet secretly expect to err again. It doesn't even fool ourselves, let alone God.

"Determination to turn away from the mistake and toward God." This is the literal meaning of *repent:* "to turn back," and it is the only mindset that readies us for his forgiveness.

Step three: Ask for forgiveness. At this point, most of your work is behind you. The rest is up to God.

If your church does not offer sacramental confession and absolution, use the following pattern. State as clearly as possible the sin you are confessing to God, admit your own personal responsibility in the matter and your sorrow about it, and ask him to forgive you. Then live through one of the following scenes in your imagination, substituting yourself for the guilty person and accepting as your own the forgiveness offered in the story:

• The Prodigal Son (Luke 15:11-32)
• The woman taken in adultery (John 8:3-11)
• The pardoning at the Crucifixion (Luke 23:34)

If you feel nothing has happened

What if we go through these steps and still feel burdened by guilt? That's the time to examine our motives in seeking forgiveness.

Here are two that in our experience lead to frustration:

The desire simply to "feel clean" again. In essence this too is based on pride. We want to restore our beautiful self-image and escape the discomfort of shame. Sometimes a marvelous "feeling" of release and renewal is indeed granted by God as part of his forgiveness, but probably not when we make this our primary objective.

The desire to avoid painful consequences. It's natural enough to want to escape the ill-effects of our misdeeds. Unhappily, the results of past actions must many times simply be lived with. If we have truly repented and received forgiveness, however, we will have the assurance of God's love as we do so.

Forgiveness now
The proper motivation for seeking forgiveness is to reestablish a broken relationship, first with God and then with others. With others this may require time, patience, and perhaps restitution. With God the relationship is reestablished just as soon as we truly repent and turn towards him.

So the test of whether or not we are forgiven is a simple one: Do I once again see God as love? For me? Personally? When your answer is yes, there is rejoicing in heaven. "I say unto you," Jesus tells us, "there is joy in the presence of the angels of God over one sinner that repenteth" (Luke 15:10). God is love—perfect, personal, unconditional. He does not want us to be mistaken about his nature a moment longer.

Elizabeth

TWO

GOD Breaks Through... When We Pray for Others

*I*ntercessory prayer: Standing with God as he blesses and guides and heals his world.

To intercede for others is to witness God in action.

It's to enjoy the greatest privilege a believer has.

*appeared originally in *The Christian Herald*
**appeared originally in *The Breakthrough Intercessor*

Sing One for Me

Maybe St. Paul could "pray without ceasing," but how can we?

Like all couples, John and I communicate in a kind of shorthand—about intercessory prayer as about any other subject. When John remarks after church, "I said one for Jim," I understand him to mean that during the service he prayed for a neighbor. "Say one for me," as he heads for his desk, means he's having problems with a manuscript and wants me to lift the project up as he works.

One evening, however, he used a different phrase. That day I was the one having trouble with a story. As John left for Thursday night choir practice, he stuck his head around the door of my study where I'd gone back to work after dinner.

"I'll sing one for you," he said.

Sing one? I thought as I watched the car taillights disappear up the driveway. Could singing in fact be prayer—specific prayer directed at a specific need?

And indeed it did seem that the story went better. . . . "Did you really keep me in mind as you sang?" I asked later.

"Absolutely," John said. As the music flowed, he'd prayed that ideas would flow for me. Breathing in, he'd asked the Spirit to give me inspiration.

Prayer acted out. Prayer woven into the events of the day. I didn't belong to the choir, but I did go to an exercise class a couple of evenings a week. Could I "jog one" for a need I knew of? What about my other nonmental activities like ironing or making beds? Instead of wool-gathering could I make these routines spurs to prayer?

So began an experiment that soon became a joyful habit: praying not just with heart and lips, but with hands and feet and everyday motions.

Not that such prayer-while-doing takes the place of a set-aside prayer time. My most focused interceding still comes in that hour before other activity begins. But with me, anyhow, once the work day started, prayer tended to get crowded out by other pressures. When a prayer request came in I'd note it on a scrap of paper or—a lot less reliably—in the back of my mind, while I waited for that elusive tranquil moment.

Today I simply take the request with me into the busy day. "Lord, my friend is waiting for the doctor's report. Every time I have a wait today—for a printout, for a phone call, in line at the post office—let me lift her time of waiting into your peace."

Often the occupation itself suggests the prayer. Preparing a meal can be a reminder of famine victims in Ethiopia. Walking, I intercede for a friend confined to a wheelchair. Driving to town this morning I prayed that the road ahead be very clear to a young woman making a career choice.

Working, playing, eating, sleeping—could all of life be gathered up and offered in continuous intercession for the needs of the world? I'm a long, long way from even approaching such a thing. But I was launched on a new adventure in prayer the night John sang one for me.

Elizabeth

A Letter to Norman Vincent Peale

Intercessory prayer was an abstract concept, until John was diagnosed as having cancer in 1957. Here's the letter he wrote three weeks later to his boss at Guideposts.

Dear Dr. Peale,

I'd like to tell you what happened after I was assigned that article on intercessory prayer.

Friday morning, September 20, started off as such an ordinary day. After breakfast we held four-year-old Donnie and one-year-old Elizabeth to the window to wave good-bye as our seven-year-old, Scott, headed off to school. Scotty had just turned the corner when Tib remembered about the ice cream.

"I meant to tell him I'd be at the ice cream counter today," she said. Mothers here in Mount Kisco take turns selling ice cream at the school cafeteria. It's just as well Tib did not tell Scotty because she never got to the cafeteria.

A few moments later I was upstairs at my typewriter. Spread out on my desk were notes I had collected during seven years as a *Guideposts* reporter. Notes on experiences that seemed to show that prayer—this disembodied mental activity—had the power actually to impact the lives of other people.

Around lunchtime the phone rang. It was my doctor.

"Can you come to the office?" he said.

"Well, of course, Doctor. When?"

"Right now."

I put the phone down, mystified. I hadn't been to the doctor in months, except for a brief session two days earlier, when he had removed a small mole from my ear.

"It's nearly midday," I called to Tib. "Why don't you come along, then I can drop you off at school?"

The first inkling we had that something was seriously wrong was when the doctor held my chair for me. He didn't hold Tib's chair; he held mine.

"I don't know how to tell you this," the doctor said. "How can I tell a young husband and father that in all probability he's going to die?"

Shock is an amazing defense, Dr. Peale. It allows us to function with perfect calm just after hearing bad news. We sat there and listened to the doctor explain that I had a malignant melanoma. We heard him say, "It's a particularly vicious kind of cancer, especially if it enters the bloodstream. Without an operation, statistics say you have one chance in nine of being alive at the end of the year. With an operation, you have one chance in three."

We said nothing at all. After a moment he went on.

"I don't want you to take my word for this. Get at least two other opinions—from Presbyterian Hospital and from Memorial."

Tib drove home to line up a babysitter while I walked across the road to the Mount Kisco Hospital to have X rays taken. I walked beneath the brightly colored autumn trees whistling. I wasn't being heroic. I really felt that way. My body's defenses had set up a wall that the news had not yet breached.

With the X rays under my arm, I walked home. I stopped and chatted idly with some workmen repairing the road. We laughed together over something; I don't remember, now, what it was. But we laughed.

That afternoon Tib and I drove into New York City. We took my biopsy slide and X rays to the huge Presbyterian Hospital where the second report came in: malignant melanoma. Immediate surgery.

By the time we got to Memorial its pathology labs were closed until Monday morning. We left the slide and X rays and drove back out to the country.

Back home we went upstairs to my office, closed the door, and turned on the air conditioner even though it was chilly in the room, because the machine made a roar that drowned out the house noises below. And there, without warning and without embarrassment, we both began to cry. It was the moment that we first let reality peep through.

Fear is such a devastating emotion! Once it had broken through our defenses, it harried us night and day. I woke up in the night and knew that I was afraid. I went about daily routines automatically; my mind elsewhere. I spent hours with Tib going over insurance, wills, finances. Between such sessions I tried to force my mind to other matters, but I could not; I was afraid.

And then, Dr. Peale, a remarkable thing happened.

On my desk sat the unfinished manuscript on intercessory prayer. In it were numerous accounts of physical disease being healed through intercession. As our friends began to hear the news, their immediate response, like the people in my notes, was to pray.

The first prayer we learned about was the one that you

said for us from your pulpit that Sunday. After that, prayer rose about us like a flood. There was prayer at Guideposts. Our assistant art director, Sal Lazzarotti, told me he almost drove off the road saying the rosary on his way home Friday after he heard the news. Did you know, Dr. Peale, that your friend, Tessie Durlach, asked her synagogue to pray?

Prayer was in the air we breathed. We were surrounded by it, submerged in it. Prayer from experienced intercessors and from people who had never tried it before. Prayer from people we knew well and from people we had never met.

I'd known the man who handles our health insurance only as a fun-loving, poker-playing businessman. To a letter summarizing our insurance coverage, he added a P.S.: "My wife and I are praying for you." A night club singer wrote that she was praying for us after work each night, and a Catholic friend who had left her church when she remarried admitted that she'd slipped into a chapel and lit a candle for me.

On Tuesday we got the report from Memorial. It confirmed the previous reports, and I was admitted there on Thursday for an operation on Friday morning.

And to my amazement the atmosphere at the hospital was one of prayer, too. No sooner had I settled down in my bed in room 609, than I was startled by a weird and haunting call, almost a cry. In the room next to mine an Orthodox patient was celebrating the Jewish New Year, Rosh Hashanah. The nurse told me I had heard the sound of the ram's horn, which for centuries has been used to summon Jews to prayer as their first act of each new year.

During that long week, what about my own prayers? They were real enough. But curiously, they were not for myself. They were for others.

I must emphasize, Dr. Peale, that I'm simply trying to

report facts. I prayed for others, not out of selflessness, but because I simply did not feel the need to pray for myself. This struck me as a little strange until I realized the reason. Suddenly, there in Memorial on the night before the operation, I was aware that I was free of fear!

Was this the tangible result of so much prayer? I think it was. That Thursday night I felt such a surge of health that I had to keep reminding myself I was in a hospital.

At six o'clock the next morning, a nurse roused me and gave me a needle. "This will make you sleepy," she said.

I laughed. Deep down. "You wake me up to give me something to make me sleep?"

They came and wheeled me into the operating room. It was as if I and the white-masked nurses and doctors were in the center of a force that dispelled fear. The closest I can come to describing it is to say that I felt as if I were deeply and personally loved.

And that, of course, must be a perfect condition for healing.

The operation was over.

There was a week of waiting. Then the doctor came into my room to give his prognosis. He didn't do it right away. He shined a light into my eyes, probed and thumped. Then, in a matter-of-fact voice: "Your report is the best one I could possibly have for you. No evidence of residual melanoma."

Does this mean I am healed?

I am not a doctor, and I do not pretend to understand the vagaries of cancer. Has it all been removed? Will it come back? Not even doctors can say. But I do know about another kind of healing; one I believe is just as important.

Before the operation I lived as I think most of us do, in a kind of twilight fear of cancer. Then, when I did get it, that fear blossomed into a monster. Fear had the power to destroy just as surely as did the melanoma.

Now I can confidently tell you, Dr. Peale, that there's been a cure. I personally have experienced the power of intercessory prayer to heal a devastating disease—the power of prayer to overcome fear.

Sincerely,
John

The Nudge

Is it merely chance when a friend is brought to mind?

Often, walking down the street or driving around town, I will see a stranger who reminds me of someone I know. Perhaps the individual actually looks like the person I am reminded of, but the trigger can be as subtle as a posture, a gesture, or a hairstyle.

In any event, for years I have put these fleeting resemblances to special use. I let my memory go to work, bringing up specifics about the person thus brought unexpectedly to mind: his voice, the last conversation we had together. Then I pray. First, briefly, for the stranger ("Bless him today"). Next for the friend I'm reminded of. I have no way of knowing my friend's particular need at that moment, of course, so I usually pray "in the Spirit," trusting that since I do not know what to ask for, the Holy Spirit intercedes for me.

Not too long ago I was reminded in this way of Leonora Wood, Catherine Marshall LeSourd's mother. Tib and I had known Mrs. Wood for a quarter of a century, and always when we visited Evergreen Farm in Virginia, she was the first person we sought out. Two specifics we especially looked forward to: her laugh and the strength of her handshake. Gradually she'd been weakened by age and illness. But her laugh and her handclasp were unchanged.

One day while Tib and I were living in Austria for a few months, I had occasion to shake hands with another elderly lady. Her grip was strong and warm, and for an instant I was back in a farmhouse in Virginia. "Thank you, Lord, for Leonora Wood. I ask your special blessing on her right at this moment." Then, as usual, I prayed for her in the Spirit.

Is there a mystic element in these nudges to intercession, or are these superficial resemblances no more than chance reminders?

There is no way of knowing, of course, but in this case I got the hint of an answer. The very next day Len LeSourd called us in Austria from Evergreen Farm. He told us that Mrs. Wood was seriously ill and asked for our prayers.

"Len," I was able to say, "your request has already been received."

John

Note: Mother Wood, at age ninety-seven, went to be with the Lord on February 19, 1989.

The Cheating Husband

In prayer God speaks to our hearts. But can prayer change the heart of someone else?

Ken Boen's rodeo act always draws a tense interest: the crowd never knows whether it is going to laugh at Ken's antics or gasp at his death.

Ken is a rodeo clown. His act has a specific reason for being. In the popular event known as bull riding, there is always a critical moment. The cinched, bucking bull is let out of his stall, a rider on his back. Within seconds, of course, the rider is thrown. The bull stops, turns, looks around, spots the rider and lowers his horns for the charge.

At this moment, Ken Boen steps between them. And there in the danger zone, dressed in top hat and tails, his face painted in a clown's broad smile, Ken Boen puts on a comedy act, drawing the bull's charge while the rider escapes. At the last possible instant, without breaking the rhythm of his act, Ken sidesteps as horn and hoof rush past.

That's the way it's supposed to go. With just an infinitesimal slip in timing, however, a rodeo clown can be killed. Many are, and even the best are often hurt. An unexpected twitch of the steer's horns, a flap of the clown's coattail—

that's all it takes. Ken has been thrown more than a hundred times, so far escaping with no more than a broken bone or two. And always, when Ken rolls away from the bull, his last gesture for the crowd is a devil-may-care grin.

"No matter how badly hurt I am," Ken says, "I can't let the audience see it." Just as he never let people see the unhappiness that used to rage inside him. For years Ken's painted smile hid an inner misery.

Ken didn't know what caused the misery.

All his life he'd wanted to be just what he was: a rodeo star. He'd bought a little mare for thirty dollars and built a successful comedy routine called "The Old Gray Mare" around her. Ken's highly paid act broke all records for return engagements at Madison Square Garden in New York. "I'd realized my dream," Ken says, "but inside I was miserable."

Ken tried to run away from his unhappiness in three ways: with daring comedy bullfighting; with carousing; with women.

"Even after I was married," Ken recalls, "I spent most of my time trying to cheat on Lynn."

Ken met Lynn at the Garden when she came to the press section for his autograph. They dated for a while, then married. It was a disaster. From the first, Ken kept trying to make a country girl out of Lynn, while Lynn tried to make a city boy out of rough, 225-pound, barn-smelling Ken Boen. After they'd been married three years, Lynn packed her bags and walked away from their beautiful fieldstone house in Ft. Smith, Arkansas.

Right there Ken and Lynn's story should have stopped, with the inevitable divorce and a fight over alimony. But as the months passed, Ken began to get letters from Lynn with a strange new quality to them. They conveyed a humility, a quietness, a sense of peace. They spoke less of parties and more of something that puzzled Ken: religion. In April 1951, after Lynn had been gone six months, she wrote that she would like to come home—if Ken would just ask her.

Reluctantly, Ken did.

On May 1, 1951, Lynn walked up the steps of their elegant home. Two hours later Ken said, "Honey, I wish you'd pack and go back to New York. I just won't be able to stay faithful to you."

Lynn didn't argue. She did something better. She went to see J. Howard Smith.

J. Howard Smith was the minister of the First Baptist Church in Ft. Smith. In his study, he listened to Lynn's story, then called a special meeting of the church's intercessory prayer group. Fourteen people showed up. On the evening of May 4, 1951, the group began to pray for Lynn's request "that Ken Boen might find Christ."

The group stayed at the church all that night. Dawn, May 5, 1951, arrived. The group continued praying. Eight o'clock. Eight-thirty. It was time to go to work, but the group continued to pray. At a quarter to nine, three of the men in the group left the church and drove to the Boens' house, where Lynn was waiting for them.

On that morning of May 5, 1951, Ken had gotten up as usual, taken a shower, shaved, and said good-bye to Lynn. "I had one thing on my mind," Ken recalls. "The date I'd set up with this pretty little Mexican."

At five minutes to nine Ken got into his car, just as the three men from the church turned into his drive. Ken recognized two of the men as his neighbors. He asked the threesome brusquely what it was they wanted, adding without waiting for an answer that he had to go.

"Ken," the third man said, "you have a nice house here, and a nice car. But, Ken, have you been saved?"

It was then that Ken recognized the third man: a local fundamentalist preacher. Ken recoiled in embarrassment at the question.

"I don't know what you mean by the word *saved*," Ken said and added that he didn't want to know, and would they please move their car because he had to be going.

Just at that moment an employee of Ken's appeared from the backyard. "Mr. Boen!" Shorty called to him. "I can't get the tractor started."

Annoyed, Ken took off around the house. The trio followed at his heels.

"Haven't you got anything better to do than hang around here, Preacher?" Ken asked when he'd gotten the tractor going.

"There's nothing more important," the man replied, "than what we're doing right now."

"Yeah. Well thanks for the visit," Ken said. "I've got to be going now." He shook hands to make the farewell official and was startled at how hard the preacher's handshake was.

It was nine-twenty. Shorty, who was also a Christian, switched off the just-repaired tractor, climbed down, and joined the little cluster of men. The backyard was quiet now. Inside the ranch house, Lynn was on her knees. Down at the First Baptist Church, the remaining members of the intercessory group were still at it. They were all thoroughly late for work by now.

And suddenly, there in Ken Boen's backyard beside the idled tractor, the preacher dropped to his knees. The two neighbors followed. Then Shorty. The four men looked up at Ken. "Won't you kneel with us, son?"

Ken recalls exactly what went through his mind at that moment: *Maybe it's the way to get rid of them. I've been down on my knees in the arena and it didn't kill me.*

Inch by inch, Ken lowered himself to his knees. Beside him the preacher was mumbling something about repenting of his sins. For the first time in quite a while, Ken thought back over the times he had resolved, unsuccessfully, to be faithful to Lynn. He thought about his life that wobbled from interest to interest, how at the top of his profession, he felt no joy.

The old, sad clown.

But like a hot knife, the thought cut into his mind of the girl he was to see that morning. "No!" Ken said half-aloud, flinging his hands in front of his face to shut out the unwelcome presence of the four men. "I'll think about these things just before I die." Then he remembered the times in the arena when he had rolled over to look up at stampeding hooves. Ken knew he might not have a chance to do much thinking when the moment came.

Ken took his hands from his face. He squinted, and looked harder. There, on the cheeks of his two neighbors, Ken saw tears. Frank, unchecked tears. Grown men crying for him.

The preacher's voice again: "Don't think you need a long time to decide, Ken. The Bible is full of men who were saved in an instant. Do you accept Jesus, Ken?"

Ken felt himself grow cold, then hot. Sweating, he brought out the words.

"I do."

That's all there was to it. "I do." But even as he spoke he felt the cords of misery drop away. It was as though he'd been trussed with an invisible lasso all his life, and the rope had suddenly loosed. It was Ken who had tears on his cheeks now.

The change that had come so abruptly—to Ken, so inexplicably—was a permanent one. He and Lynn reaffirmed their marriage vows and set out to share their new happiness with others, traveling thousands of miles between rodeo engagements to hold revival meetings.

In Ken's backyard that day the three visitors knew only that they'd fulfilled Lynn's request for prayer. The preacher got up. The neighbors got up. Shorty climbed back on the tractor.

And at nine-thirty on the morning of May 5, 1951, a group of intercessors filed out of the First Baptist Church of Ft. Smith, Arkansas, and headed to work.

John and Elizabeth

The Bind

He was an obnoxious, overbearing character, and he needed prayer.

Our telephone rang one evening with news that a member of our church was filing for bankruptcy. Apparently Art was taking his business failure pretty hard. "You know how depressed Art can get," the man on the phone was saying. "Pray for him, will you?"

Of course I said I'd pray. I meant it, too. We have an informal intercessory prayer chain at church, which we take seriously.

Which made it all the more difficult for me, then, when I found I had trouble keeping my promise. As soon as I began to pray for Art (I have, of course, changed both his name and the situation he faced) my mind wandered into business problems of my own. I tried to force my attention back, but the effort backfired. All I recalled was a condescending stout little man who had a way of making me mad.

The trouble was that I was being asked to pray for a man I just did not like.

This created a peculiar problem for me as it often does, no doubt, for anyone interested in intercession. Up until that

prayer request I'd handled my dislike for Art by simply keeping my distance: if I saw him coming in one door I slipped
out of the other.

Suddenly, now, I could no longer run away. I was in a
bind; I could not pray effectively for Art, but because of my
commitment I could not avoid thinking about him either.

I was struggling with this dilemma when Tib and I had
Sunday brunch with a new acquaintance, a remarkable
woman who gave me a brace of tools for dealing with the
dilemma of how to pray for someone you don't like.

As we stood in line at the Holiday Inn buffet, we
learned that Sylvia Harmon had lost her young husband
when their children were two and four years old. Armed with
a degree as a registered nurse, Sylvia saw her daughter
through Columbia Medical School and was watching with
satisfaction as her son completed his graduate work in archi-
tecture at Harvard.

It was Sylvia's experience as an R.N. that turned out to
be so helpful to me. We'd asked, as we often do with people
in different fields, what she found to be the hardest part of
her profession. "That's easy," she said. "It's when you have
to nurse people you don't like."

I was all ears. I told Sylvia about the similar problem I
faced in intercessory prayer. "It's difficult," I said, "to pray
for people who are repulsive."

"I know," said Sylvia. "And the trouble is, we feel guilty
because we're supposed to pray for spiteful people."

As we ate, Sylvia gave Tib and me two examples from
her own career of people who had used her despitefully. She
once had a lawyer patient who had been shot in the head and
as a result suffered a personality change. He would shout
obscenities at the nurses. "I felt dirty when I walked out of
that man's room," Sylvia said.

"And there was a wealthy woman I once nursed on private duty," she recalled as she finished her meal. "She had only a few weeks to live—it was melanoma—and yet she wanted to be sure she got her money's worth out of her nurses. She couldn't bear to see me sit down. I had to be in motion for eight hours. If I so much as slowed my pace she was asking for a Kleenex or a cup of tea."

The question, of course, was how to handle it. How did Sylvia deal with the problem in this most intercessory of professions?

Two principles, she said, had helped her. First, when she was still a student in the school of nursing at Howard University, she had been trained to be impartial. "We were taught," she said, "to treat all patients with the same caring, regardless of personal inclination." Impartiality. That is the way God treats us. "He causes his sun to rise on the evil and the good, and sends rain on the righteous and the unrighteous" (Matthew 5:45, NIV).

"The second principle is harder," said Sylvia, "but even more helpful. I must remember that I am here to nurse, not to judge." This concept too is based on the way God deals with us. "The Father judges no one, but has entrusted all judgment to the Son" (John 5:22, NIV).

"There's a bonus that comes from applying these two yardsticks," Sylvia said. "Once you stop judging you are free to understand. How much truth there is in the old cliché that to understand all is to forgive all! The lawyer who shouted at me knew he'd never again be clear of mind. I'd rail, too, wouldn't you? And the woman dying of cancer—she had no belief in an afterlife. She was saying she wanted to live and hoped she would continue to need her money."

After our brunch with Sylvia Harmon, I once again thought about Art and his business crisis—and felt ashamed of my judgmentalism. We can be realistic and clear-eyed about flawed human nature, yes. But to *judge* to the point where we cannot intercede? Even the Father did not do that. He left judgment to the Son, and the reason seems clear: Jesus himself walked through the rejections and temptations of humanity and could identify with our weaknesses.

He had been there. He knew. To understand all is to forgive all. Within moments I found that I was able to begin a fresh kind of intercession for Art, trusting at the same time that when others interceded for me they could find it in themselves not to judge me first.

John

The Unexpected Answer

Leopold Mozart's prayer for his son was never granted.
Or was it?

Like the other visitors to No. 9 Getreidegasse, I was thinking as I followed the guide up the flights of dimly lit steps, about the January day in 1756 when the greatest of all musical geniuses was born in this house in Salzburg. It was not of the child I was thinking, however, nor of his mother. I was thinking of the fear-haunted man who had hurried down these same dark steps to summon the midwife.

Fear, by the time he was thirty-seven, was habitual for Leopold Mozart. Most of the time it was fear of poverty—and with reason. Leopold was a musician in a day when such men had only one way to earn a living: the service of some wealthy lord. Leopold was a composer and a violinist—that is to say, a servant—at the court of the Prince-Archbishop of Salzburg. But that was no guarantee for the future. Who knew how many musicians the next archbishop would employ?

Since coming to live in Salzburg, I'd learned more about this man who seemed in some ways so like people of our own day. His wish for security, for instance. It was a strange notion in an age when ordinary men lived at the whim of the rich and powerful. But Leopold had many strange ideas. Another, in a rational and unbelieving age, was that God could answer prayer. Leopold's prayer was a very specific one: he wanted to be appointed chief musician of the archbishop's household. Then, no matter who ruled in Salzburg, he felt his position would be safe.

We'd arrived at the third-floor apartment where Leopold Mozart had brought his bride, Anna Maria, in 1747. "This is the birth chamber," intoned the tour guide, stopping at a room just big enough to hold a rope-strung bed and a table with a pitcher and bowl.

The group moved on, but I lingered behind, imagining Leopold's anxiety on that January day. At thirty-six, Anna Maria was past the age when women were supposed to bear children. Childbirth was risky enough at best. Six times in this little room Anna Maria had survived the ordeal—only to watch five children die in infancy.

"We have Nanneri," her husband would have tried to console her. At age four their one surviving child was showing such musical talent that Leopold had already started giving the little girl lessons on the clavichord.

In this small back room that winter night, Anna Maria delivered a seventh child, a son. Before illness could claim him too, Leopold hurried him to the cathedral to be baptized Wolfgang Gottlieb, Wolfgang Beloved-by-God.

But this child surprised his parents by surviving the croups and fevers of his first two winters to become a lively toddler. A toddler who listened transfixed to Nanneri's clavichord lessons. Who by age three was clambering onto the bench to reproduce note for note the melodies he had heard.

Looking on in surprise, Leopold realized that he and Anna Maria had a second musical prodigy under their roof. He began giving Wolfgang keyboard lessons, too, marveling at the speed with which he learned. When the little boy was six a family friend presented him with a half-sized violin which he carried with him everywhere. One evening his father and two friends were rehearsing a string trio in the large front room at No. 9 Getreidegasse, when Wolfgang piped up: "Father, I would like to play, too!"

The visitors chuckled, but Leopold was embarrassed: well-mannered children did not speak in the presence of adults. "Go to your mother!" he said. "We are working."

"I could play second violin," Wolfgang persisted.

"Don't talk nonsense!" his father exploded. "You haven't had violin lessons. Leave the room at once!"

Eyes brimming, Wolfgang started for the door. "It doesn't take lessons," the men heard him murmur, "to play second violin."

Leopold could never bear to see a child cry. "All right," he said gruffly, "stand beside Herr Schachtner and pretend to play—but softly so you don't distract us."

Schachtner, playing second violin, watched the little boy bowing away beside him with amusement . . . which swiftly changed to wonder. Gradually it was Herr Schachtner who played softer and softer. And Leopold who wept. His son, he was beginning to grasp, was not just a prodigy, but a miracle of God.

Miracles, of course, were scoffed at in that Age of Enlightenment; educated people no longer believed in God. But Leopold did believe, and to him his duty was clear. To a "rational" world he must exhibit the boy's gifts, which no amount of rationalizing could explain.

It would mean obtaining a leave-of-absence from the archbishop, weakening his claim to that secure top post. But if they traveled for the honor of God, surely he would see to their support?

Accompanied by their proud parents, Wolfgang and Nanneri performed at court after brilliant court. At six Wolfgang played for the Empress of Austria, at seven for the King of France, at eight for the royalty of England. The child passed every test his incredulous hearers could devise. He sight-read complicated scores. From another room he named notes struck at random on the clavichord; with a single hearing reproduced long pieces from memory. One baffled Englishman sent to Salzburg for the boy's birth certificate to be sure he was not a midget adult.

The only thing the tours failed to produce was enough income even to cover expenses. Watches, snuffboxes, miniature portraits of the great nobles for whom the children played . . . trinkets were pressed on them in abundance. But little else—and Leopold's fears for the future redoubled.

Between tours Leopold labored to make up the missed time with his employer. By now Wolfgang could not only play any instrument in the orchestra, but had started composing songs, quartets, symphonies, even opera. Leopold was a good enough composer to know that his son's music showed not talent but genius—genius of an order he'd never imagined.

By thirteen, Wolfgang had absorbed all that his father could teach him. And now came an invitation to visit Italy, center of the musical world. At eighteen, Nanneri was past the age when respectable females could perform in public. So father and son set off alone.

This new leave-of-absence, Leopold knew, ruined once and for all his chance of promotion. But by now, his own future forgotten, it was his son's security he prayed for. Surely, having given him supernatural gifts of creation, God would also provide a generous patron who would allow Wolfgang to use those gifts in tranquility?

The two Mozarts arrived in Rome at Easter, in time to hear Allegri's *Miserere* performed in the Sistine Chapel. This immense nine-part choral work was the Chapel's exclusive property: copies were issued only to performers, who were threatened with excommunication if they showed so much as a bar of it to anyone else. The thirteen-year-old visitor from Salzburg knew nothing of this regulation. But he enjoyed the performance and when he got back to his hotel room he jotted it down, all nine parts of the entire lengthy score.

When his manuscript was discovered there was scandal. Then the truth came out: the Pope himself awarded the *wunderkind* the Order of the Golden Spur, and in acknowledgment Wolfgang changed his middle name, Gottlieb, to its Latin equivalent, Amadeus.

Though father and son did not know it, this was to be the pattern for the next ten years. In foreign courts, honors and adulation, but nothing to live on. In Salzburg no recognition, but a steady if inadequate income.

For Wolfgang too was now in the archbishop's employ, playing violin in his orchestra and the organ for cathedral services, turning out settings for the mass and divertimenti to accompany the great man's meals. The mediocre performances his works received were a torture to the teenage genius, who by now had heard the finest orchestras of Europe. Yet when he sat down to compose, masterpieces flowed from him. Frustrated though he was, he could turn out nothing second rate. That, Leopold knew, was because it was God himself who made music through his son.

Therefore God would provide security! Over and over Leopold wrote to the influential people they'd met on their tours, appealing to them to find his son a suitable post. A number of promising replies came back, and in 1777 the twenty-one-year-old set out to audition once more at various courts.

This time, however, Leopold was not with him. The old archbishop of Salzburg had died; his replacement, the haughty Count Colleredo, was not about to let *two* of his servants go skylarking around Europe. The younger Mozart he grudgingly allowed to go, but Leopold must stick to his duties. Leopold, nearing sixty, knew he would have no job at all if he disobeyed.

And so it was Anna Maria who accompanied their son on the new round of court visits. An endless stream of letters from Leopold followed them. The Elector Karl Theodore of Mannheim, Leopold wrote, was rich and generous; a position with him would guarantee Wolfgang's future! What the anxious father did not see was that the security he wanted for his son was already coming about—though not in the way Leopold envisioned.

"Let come what will," Wolfgang wrote back as he waited in Mannheim. "Nothing can go ill so long as it is the will of God."

Here was tranquility indeed! Tranquility that through each crushed hope (the Elector turned down Wolfgang's application) nevertheless allowed the most glorious music the world had yet heard to flow day after day from his pen.

A far greater test lay just ahead. In March 1778 Wolfgang and his mother arrived in Paris and took the best accommodation they could afford; a small dark room above a scrap iron dealer, where the rain seeped through the walls.

Anna Maria fell ill. Admirers of Wolfgang's music found better lodgings for them, but the damage had been done. Week by week the young man watched his beloved mother grow worse. Yet it was the joy of heaven, not the anguish of earth, that continued to sing through his music.

Wolfgang revealed his secret in the letter he wrote his father from Paris. "I am convinced that no doctor, no man, no accident, can either give life to man or take it away. That rests with God alone."

God alone. Almost without knowing it, Leopold had communicated his unfashionable faith as well as his solid musicianship. "She is not lost to us forever," Wolfgang wrote in his letter that broke the news of Anna Maria's death. "We shall see her again. We shall be together more joyous and happy than ever we were in this world."

This world indeed proved an unwelcoming place for this man of genius. The financial security his father wanted for him was never granted. All his short life Wolfgang scrounged to make ends meet, scrambling to support a wife and family, never sure where the next month's rent would come from.

And yet . . . God had answered a father's prayer better than he knew. Wolfgang wrote these words to him a month before Leopold's death and four years before Mozart's own, at the age of thirty-five: "I never go to sleep, young as I am, without thinking that I may never see the following day. Yet nobody can call me melancholy. . . . Death is the real aim of our life. How I thank my God for the bliss of knowing him as the key to true happiness!"

Surely, I thought, as I headed back down the stairs from that Salzburg apartment, Leopold's wish had been granted more fully than he dreamed. In his concern for his son, Leopold had been thinking of worldly security. Wolfgang, swifter than his father to learn spiritual truths as well as musical ones, had discovered the security that lasts forever.

Elizabeth

The Penny Prayer

How can we keep prayer from becoming problem-centered?

Before going to sleep that Monday night I reached for my Bible. John had asked for prayer about a business trip, and whenever I tried to pray without the aid of Scripture, my thoughts were invariably bogged down on the problems. There were plenty of those in the current situation.

Earlier that day John had flown out to Grand Rapids, Michigan, where the next day, Tuesday, September 6, 1982, he would take part in merger talks between our small publishing company, Chosen Books, and a large corporation. But what about the particular kind of Christian publishing we believed God had called us to? Could it survive such a merger? What about the Chosen staff in Lincoln, Virginia? Some of them had moved families there, bought homes. Would they be uprooted? Lose their jobs?

"Pray!" John had said as he left for the airport. And so I opened the Bible and once again watched the familiar phenomenon take place: my thoughts channeled by Scripture away from mere anxiety and into authentic intercession.

The decisive meeting, out in Michigan, was to begin the

following day at two o'clock. That was the hour when John and our partner, Len LeSourd, would be sitting down with the officers of the Zondervan Corporation.

As it happened I, too, had a trip scheduled for Tuesday, a drive to upstate New York. It was a beautiful early autumn day and my route was a spectacular one through the Catskill Mountains. About midday I passed an irresistible wooden signpost: "Escarpment Trail."

I parked the car in the rest area and set out on foot up the mountainside. The path climbed through a pine and oak forest so silent and splendid that by the time I looked at my watch it was already two o'clock, the hour I'd assured John I'd be remembering him and Len in Grand Rapids. About a hundred yards off the trail I spotted a low outcropping of rock. I worked my way to it through the tangled branches, sat down, and closed my eyes.

But instead of intercession, what came into my mind in that whispering silence beneath the pines was a string of self-accusations. Maybe God had never wanted us to get into publishing in the first place. Or maybe he had—still did. Maybe this merger idea was only our own wishful way out of the cash flow problems created by the past year's recession.

I knew, of course, that this kind of fretting was not prayer. But my Bible, which could have put these issues into perspective, was in the car miles away at the foot of the mountain. How could I stop my mind from running in problem-centered circles? How could I really, meaningfully, hold up the men meeting in Grand Rapids?

I opened my eyes.

And blinked.

On the ground, not two feet away, lay a bright copper penny. I reached down and picked it up. How a shiny new coin came to be lying on that remote mountain slope a hundred yards from the trail, I could not imagine. I sat staring at it as though it were the first penny I'd ever seen.

Lincoln's profile. Arching over his head were the words: In God we trust. Below, *1982* and the word *Liberty.*

Why, I wasn't holding just a penny! Here were the themes for my prayer.

In God we trust. Not in our skill at negotiating. The welfare of our employees, the books we were to publish, God had the answers to these concerns! "This afternoon in Grand Rapids, Father, let Len and John take a new step in trusting you."

1982. He wasn't the God of a distant past or an imaginary future; he was God of the present moment. "Father, show Len and John your will, for now, for this situation."

Liberty. Freedom for the captives—of any and every kind—was always the will of God. "Father, release Len and John to use the skills you've given them—to work with words and not with numbers."

And those whose skills were different, those with God's gifts of business management and marketing: "Father, let the decisions in Grand Rapids mean new liberty for them as well."

God. Trust. Liberty. My penny prayer went on so long that I became conscious of the hard rock beneath me. Three words in Latin on the reverse side of the coin caught my attention as I stood up: *E pluribus unum:* "out of many, one." Was God telling me with a chuckle that the merger *was* his answer, that out of these two companies a single one was to emerge?

That was, as it turned out, the result of the deliberations that afternoon in Grand Rapids. The merger of Zondervan and Chosen Books permitted us to maintain our staff in Lincoln and pursue our particular philosophy of publishing.

I didn't know this as I hiked back down the mountain that September afternoon with a penny in my pocket. I only knew I had a secret to intercession, anywhere I found myself. God has filled the world with clues to his presence; the humblest object can remind us that he's in charge.

Elizabeth

"Someone's in Trouble!"

She felt a vague uneasiness, an undefined sense of impending disaster.

The sky was overcast as Hermano Pablo and four other Christian ministers climbed into Pablo's ancient Chevrolet. For a week they'd been conducting revival meetings in a rural area of El Salvador; now they were heading back to San Salvador, the country's capital.

The trip over the narrow, twisting roads was hazardous even under good weather conditions, and conditions that morning were far from good. It was the rainy season in El Salvador, and in many places the dirt roads had turned to mud. Worse, none of the five men in the car knew this region. They did not know that 150 miles ahead of them, around a blind curve, lay the tracks of a railway.

That same morning, many miles away in the city of Santa Ana, an Indian housemaid was having trouble settling down to work. Angela Mancía kept stopping in the middle of her chores.

Angela worked for a missionary couple, Ralph and Jewel Williams. She knew Hermano Pablo well (he always stayed with the Williams when he was in Santa Ana), and

Angela often prayed for him and his work. But she was not thinking about him that morning. Indeed, she was having trouble thinking about anything much. Her thoughts kept being disturbed by a vague uneasiness, an undefined sense of impending disaster.

Meanwhile, Hermano Pablo was driving with one eye on the thunderclouds massing in the east. His friends too—Israel García beside him in the front seat, and Juan, José, and Fernando in the back—watched the approaching storm as they talked.

About eleven o'clock the rain reached them, the tropical storm lashing the windshield faster than the wipers could sweep it clean. Pablo leaned forward, straining to see ahead.

Angela was struggling with unaccountable tears when Jewel Williams walked into the kitchen. "Angela! What on earth's the matter?"

"I don't know, señora," Angela said. "Except . . . " and all at once she was sure of something. "Someone's in trouble! I know it! Do you think . . . do you think I should go up to the church and pray?"

Jewel thought she should. So Angela started up the muddy street to the little church where she and the Williams family worshipped.

Ordinarily it took about ten minutes to climb the hill. But that morning it took Angela half an hour because she stopped to talk to every Christian friend she met. To each she described the strange uneasiness, the growing sureness that God was telling her to pray for someone.

"Won't you come with me?" she asked each one. Half a dozen women did. And so it was that just before midday a handful of Indian Christians walked through the door of the little Assembly of God church, sat down, and began to pray without knowing what it was they were praying about.

At about one o'clock the five ministers stopped in a small town for lunch. Outside, the rain continued. The roads were growing more slippery every minute. But the five men had commitments in San Salvador. They climbed back into the old car and went on.

In Santa Ana, the pendulum clock on the wall of the church read one-thirty. The women prayed without stopping to eat, unaware of hunger; unaware of anything except the urgency that now gripped them all. "Lord, somewhere one of your children is in trouble. You know who it is, Lord Jesus. Put your hand where the need is."

With the rain hammering on the car roof, Pablo thought it was like driving inside a drum. It was nearly as dark as the inside of a drum, too, though it was only two in the afternoon. Pablo decided to stop until the storm was over. But where? Just ahead he made out a curve. Beyond it, perhaps there'd be a place to pull over.

"Be with your child, Lord, wherever he is!"

"Look out!" Israel García cried.

The headlight of a train loomed from nowhere out of the storm. Pablo jerked the wheel and slammed on the brakes, but the car kept sliding over the mud.

They heard the frantic scream of the whistle. Then the locomotive hit them. The car spun around, and the train hit it again. The right-hand door flew open; Garcia was hurled out. The car rose into the air and came down on its roof.

"Help your child, Lord!" the women prayed.

Pablo opened his eyes. The rain had stopped, and he was lying on the ground, surrounded by a group of people. On the railway track was a tangle of metal that only gradually he recognized as his Chevrolet.

Now he realized that he must be delirious, because it seemed to him that among the crowd were his four friends—

all alive and all talking to a policeman, who was making notes in a little book. The engineer of the train was there, too, staring at them.

At a question from the policeman, the engineer drew a watch from his pocket. In the voice of one dazed, he replied, "It's two-thirty."

Pablo felt himself for broken bones, then gingerly got to his feet. "It's not possible!" the engineer cried. Pablo was being embraced by Juan, José, Fernando, and Israel. At the policeman's orders, though they kept assuring him they were all right, the five started for the ambulance, away from the circle of gaping passengers, away from the still throbbing locomotive, away from the sound of the engineer's voice repeating, "It's not possible! No one could have walked away from that car!"

Far away in Santa Ana, the prayer vigil was over. A sudden silence fell over the church. Angela opened her eyes and looked around. The haunted feeling was gone.

The other women felt it, too. They knew that whatever they had been called to do was now accomplished.

For the first time Angela remembered the work waiting for her back at the house. She glanced at the pendulum clock on the church wall and was astonished to see how late it was. The clock's hands stood at two-thirty.

John and Elizabeth

How to Live with Your Prayer Life

"Please pray for my husband . . . ," ". . . our youth work in the inner city," ". . . Christians in China . . ." Day after day appeals for prayer bombard us.

As I was clearing out my briefcase some time ago I ran across a slip of paper reading: "Pray for Fred, one o'clock." My friend's job interview had been two whole days ago and had completely slipped my mind. I was distressed because once again I had promised I would pray, and then I'd forgotten.

Another time I was talking with a popular Christian speaker who receives a dozen prayer requests a day in his California home. "I sometimes wonder if people know what they're asking," he said. "Prayer takes energy and time. It takes the very best of ourselves." He tries, I know, to hold up each need, but confesses that many of these prayers are perfunctory and thus a source of guilt for him.

And at our own church in Mount Kisco, New York, where much intercession is offered, no formal prayer list is kept for an interesting reason. "When do you take someone's name off?" our rector explained. "No one likes to think that prayer for him has stopped."

These three problems, then, are common to everyone

who prays for others. We promise to pray at a particular time, but the phone rings and we forget. We wish we could pray for every need we hear of, but we quickly discover our own limitations. And we wonder if it is ever permitted to lay down a concern we have lifted.

I had been struggling with these questions for some time when I came across two concepts which, combined, have changed my intercessory prayer pattern and I think can be helpful to others.

1. Prayer on the spot

Some years ago I was facing a complex decision about an employee. One day, while I was fretting over it, I had a call from a friend and publisher, Dan Malachuk. When he asked how things were, I shared with him the problem I was facing.

"Let's pray about it right now," Dan said. And together over the phone we did pray for the situation. Dan did not say, "I'll keep you in my prayers," or, "Viola and I will be praying for you," or any of the other phrases that spring so glibly to our lips. Instead, then and there, he joined me in my concern. It meant a great deal to me, and I am sure went far to help resolve the dilemma I was in.

Since then I have borrowed this practice of on-the-spot prayer. When a request comes to my attention, I stop whatever I am doing and pray about the matter right then. Sometimes the prayer is said aloud with the other person participating. Other times, for example, if the request has come in a letter I'm answering, I stop typing and pray, and tell my correspondent that I have done so. In either case the point is the same: I pray before I have a chance to forget.

I do not, however, promise further involvement unless the following second stage occurs.

2. Prayer at the Spirit's prompting

This idea comes from the book *Rees Howells: Intercessor,* by our friend Norman Grubb. Grubb's book is a biography of a man who gave his life to the task of praying for others—with remarkable results. One of the secrets Howells learned early was this: He was not supposed to intercede in depth for every situation that came to his attention; he was to pray only for those needs that were given to him by the Holy Spirit.

I suddenly saw that this made a great deal of sense. Doubtless, in God's ecology, each Christian will be given by the Spirit just a handful of people for whom he is to intercede with special concentration. Even Jesus, with limitless prayer resources, had to be selective; the pool of Bethesda had five porches filled with disabled people; yet Jesus healed only one.

So this, too, I have incorporated into my intercessory prayer life. Now, in addition to praying on the spot for a need that has been pointed out to me, I also make a promise. "I will pray for this situation," I say, "as often as the Holy Spirit brings it to my mind."

I consider this a real commitment and try to be obedient. I pause wherever I am and lift up the concern that is given to me at that moment by the Spirit.

As I have explored this approach to intercessory prayer, I have found it to carry two benefits:

First, I no longer personally have to carry the burden of remembering a particular person at a particular time. In the process I've been released from the feeling I sometimes had before, that intercessory prayer was a chore, a matter of watching the clock and feeling anxious—as though the effect of the prayer depended on *me* and on *my* faithfulness.

Second, I find that I am getting used to praying a lot more often than before. Perhaps three times as much. I am astonished at how effortlessly I can stop whatever I am doing and pray for the need that springs into my consciousness. Intercessory prayer now fits into the rhythm of the day rather than into a schedule that I try to impose.

I have a feeling that in some mysterious way these promptings to pray make the intercessions not my own, but Christ's. They are his prayers, offered through a member of his body in his perfect time (how often I have discovered that the timing of my Spirit-prompted prayer coincided precisely with a moment of crisis!) and for needs that perhaps are known to him alone.

John

Three

GOD Breaks Through... in Silence

We cultivate noise. From the clanging of the alarm clock until we snap off the late-night TV, we wrap ourselves in an intentional barrage of sound. In our century silence has come to seem unnatural: proof of failure in company . . . threatening when alone.

Yet it is in silence that the voice of God speaks to the human heart. "Be still and know that I am God." If we learn to be still, what knowledge will come into that holy hush?

The Condolence Call

He was a famous preacher. He would be able to put into words all that we could not.

A heavy snow was falling that January night as we drove toward New York City, where John's father had died of a heart attack an hour earlier. *What can we possibly say to Mother at such a time?* we wondered in the midst of our own shock.

It was one o'clock in the morning when we took the elevator up to their flat at Union Theological Seminary, where Dad had taught. After dinner that evening, Mother told us, they'd gone for a walk in the snow. Two hours later, Dad complained of pain in his chest. The doctor had arrived too late.

We groped for words of comfort, but none came. At last the three of us went to bed.

The following morning the doorbell rang at seven. I pulled a bathrobe around me, opened the door, and sighed with relief. Standing in the hallway was Reinhold Niebuhr. A fellow professor at Union, this renowned theologian was well-versed in the mysteries of life and death. He would be able to put into words all that we could not.

I led Dr. Niebuhr into the living room and went to call John and his mother. We all took chairs while I waited eagerly to hear the words of Christian insight Dr. Niebuhr would pronounce. A minute passed . . . two minutes . . . while my expectation mounted. At last, with crooked arthritic fingers, he reached for Mother's hand.

"Well, Helen," he said—the very first words he had uttered.

Silence fell again. Five minutes . . . ten full minutes elapsed, and still this gifted preacher had not shared his words of wisdom.

After fifteen minutes, the stillness of the room began to seep inside me as a wordless communication enfolded us all. When the clock chimed the half hour, Dr. Niebuhr stood up and let himself out.

And still John, Mother, and I sat silent. Not until the undertakers arrived just before eight did any of us speak, and then only to deal with the logistics of death. Later John and I would find the words of love and honoring that need to be spoken in their time.

For now, though, it was enough that we were there.

We had learned the power of silence from one of the great speakers of our century. Niebuhr had not come with words, no matter how lofty. He had brought instead the best, the costliest thing one person can give to another. He had brought himself. And in silence now the three of us reached for the presence of one another . . . and of God.

Elizabeth

The Secret of the Bench

Does God have a plan for your life?

In the early 1950s millions of Americans, glancing through their newspapers at the ads for soap and cigarettes, stumbled across another kind of selling copy. Sandwiched between the commercial promotions was an advertisement urging a return to religion. Down in the corner of the ad, in ultra-small type, were the words, *Keister Advertising Service, Strasburg, Virginia.*

The story behind the ads began with a green wooden bench . . . .

Earl Keister was a restless young man. In dot-on-the map Strasburg, times were hard. So bad that about the time he got married Strasburg's weekly newspaper was offered to anyone who would promise to pay its debts. Keister took the challenge.

Strasburg's population of two thousand, he soon realized, was too small to support a separate paper. With his bride, Arline, he borrowed money, purchased the ailing weeklies of six neighboring towns, and consolidated them into the *Northern Virginia Daily.* With the wider distribution, the paper began at last to prosper.

And with prosperity, the restlessness returned.

Looking around for new challenges, Keister ventured into the advertising business, doing promotions for the regional chamber of commerce, designing war bond ads during the Second World War. Here were broader horizons. Yet, Keister wondered, where was it all heading?

And then he built the bench.

Keister and his wife had bought a farm just outside Strasburg. Overlooking their property there's a steep bluff with a magnificent view over the Shenandoah Valley. Keister started coming to the bluff when he had a problem he couldn't solve. The bench he built there isn't much to look at: rough hewn, splintered, painted park bench green. But it changed his life.

In Sigrid Undset's "The Cross," there's a passage that describes what happened at the bench: "When man comes up on a height above his native place, and looks down from it into his own dale . . . he knows each farm and fence, each thicket, the gully of each beck; but he seems to see for the first time how these things all lie on the face of the land."

This was the secret of the bench: perspective. Soon, a trip to the bench became as necessary to Keister's day as sleep. Usually nothing spectacular would happen. He would sit in silence, meditating, musing, praying.

One evening, after a particularly hard business day, Earl Keister went to his bench with three pieces of paper in his hand. He had a sense of excitement, as though he were on the verge of discovering, at last, a direction and pattern to his life. There, overlooking the valley, he spread the papers before him: a copy of the newspaper, a proof of the latest bond ad, and a church bulletin. They were the summation of his life, and suddenly he saw that they formed a unity. Newspapers. Advertising. Church. Why not combine the three: create a "Support the Church" advertising service for newspapers?

Keister took a survey of church attendance and discovered that there was a desperate need for the right kind of campaign. Half the country had no religious affiliation; of the other half, millions were church members in name only.

Keister consulted with others on newspapers and in church groups. Everyone agreed that the ads should avoid denominational bias. Rather than a reproachful, guilt-inducing approach, they should stress the benefits of church attendance. They should be written for the nonchurched, using the techniques of modern advertising—visual appeal, catchy heads, brief to-the-point copy—all aimed at the central idea: rediscover your own religion.

In August 1944 Keister placed his first ad in the Charleston, West Virginia, *Gazette*. Six months later twelve papers were taking his ads, costs covered by community leaders in each area. Most important to Keister were letters from readers: "I've decided to give religion a try," or, "I'd grown away from my childhood faith and rediscovered it through your advertisements." Encouraged, Keister kept going. Within five years he was employing twenty people full time, placing hundreds of ads in 700 newspapers.

Those same five years saw the beginning of what is now recognized as a national resurgence of religion in the post–Second World War years. Keister would be the last person on earth to claim that his ads brought this about. He does believe, however, that God had a plan for those years, and that he was able to be part of that plan because of a green bench on a bluff.

The bench, the place apart where we go to seek the larger picture, is not a new idea. The financier and statesman Bernard Baruch found a bench in New York City's Central

Park, where he sat musing for long, silent hours. Theodore Roosevelt, another park-bencher, used the time to bring perspective to his job as president.

But of course, as Keister pointed out in his ads, the most famous type of bench is the church pew. No one will ever be able to put into statistics the millions of people who have found perspective there.

Like Earl Keister, each one of us is being groomed by our specific life experiences for our part in God's master plan. All that is needed in addition is a bench where we can sit and see the divine pattern unfold.

John

A Strange Kind of Laziness

"I hope," the poet said, "you won't ask me for definitions."

The poet, dressed in a gray suit and white shirt open at the neck, was finishing breakfast. His first words were keynotes. Robert Frost looked up, shaggy white eyebrows rising. "I hope you won't ask me to put names on things," he said. "I'm afraid of that."

But of course that was just what we had come to do. *God*, for instance. What did this word mean to him in such poems as "Bereft," written after the death of his wife?

> Where had I heard this wind before
>> Change like this to a deeper roar? . . .
>
> Something sinister in tone
>> Told me my secret must be known:
>
> Word I was in the house alone
>> Somehow must have gotten abroad,
>
> Word I was in my life alone,
>> Word I had no one left but God.

Frost folded his massive hands and spoke with the same subtle indirection that pervades his poetry. "People have sometimes asked me to sum up my poetry. I can't do that. It's the same with my feeling about God. If you would learn the way a man feels about God, don't ask him to put names to it. All that is said with names is soon not enough.

"If you would have out the way a man feels about God," he continued, "watch his life, hear his words. Place a coin, denomination unknown, beneath a piece of paper, and you can discover what it is by rubbing a pencil over the paper. From all the individual rises and valleys your answer will come out."

We reviewed what we knew about Frost's life. Perhaps from its rises and valleys a picture would emerge.

Robert Frost was born in 1875 in San Francisco, three thousand miles from the New England he wrote about. Frost's family, however, were ninth generation New Englanders, and when his father died, Frost's mother moved with her son back to Lawrence, Massachusetts, to live with her in-laws.

It was while Frost was living with his grandparents that he bought his first book of poetry. Spending money was at a minimum, so the boy would visit bookshops and browse. "I'd gone to Cambridge one day," he recalled, "and was standing in a bookshop thumbing through Francis Thompson's famous poem, *The Hound of Heaven*. I became fascinated with his idea that we are not seeking God, but God is seeking us. I bought the book. I spent my return fare on it and had to walk home."

The distance was twenty-five miles!

It was in Massachusetts, too, that Robert Frost wrote his first poem. No English was taught at his school. Only history, mathematics, and Greek. In history class one day, Frost learned about Cortez, the Spanish conqueror of Mexico. Walking home that afternoon, he composed a long ballad about Cortez.

"I remember the time so clearly," said Frost. "I recall that there was a wind and darkness. I had never written a poem before, and as I walked, it appeared like a revelation, and I became so wrapped up in it that I was late to my grandmother's. The next day I took it to the editor of our school paper and it was published."

Nothing was quite the same for Robert Frost after that. It isn't that he suddenly had a burning ambition to become a great poet. It was more of a recognition, a knowledge that he would go on writing poems even if it led to difficulties.

The difficulties were not long in coming. It was apparent to those close to Frost that something had happened. The teenage boy seemed to have lost all ambition. His grandfather thought he was plain lazy and began pressuring him to get settled into some respectable work.

Reflecting on those days, Frost recalled that no one had confidence in his future. "Where is it that confidence and faith separate?" he asked. "We have confidence in the atom. We can test the atom and prove that it is there. I have seen an old New England farmer try to test God in this same way. He stood in his field during a thunderstorm and held his pitchfork to heaven and dared God to strike him. You just can't prove God that way."

Robert Frost couldn't have had confidence in his poetry. He submitted it to magazines time and again and most of it was returned. But he did have faith in it.

Meanwhile the pressure continued to pin Frost down, to get him to commit himself to a career. His grandfather got him a job as a bobbin boy in one of the textile mills in Lawrence, hoping he would rise through the ranks. Frost took the work, but he refused to advance. He spent the nights writing.

About this time Frost married his childhood sweetheart, Elinor White. His grandfather bought them a farm up in

New Hampshire, but Frost refused to fit into the expected mold there either. Reports began to circulate among the neighbors that young Frost milked his cows late at night so he wouldn't have to get up early in the morning. Frost was writing poetry most of the night and needed the sleep. But others called it laziness.

To provide support for his growing family, Frost took a teaching job there in New Hampshire. The school was impressed by the popularity of Frost's unorthodox classes, where students were expected to catch the *spirit* of the subject matter, not a series of facts. When Frost was thirty-six, the job of headmaster became vacant. Frost was offered the position.

At last, in the eyes of friends and family, Frost was on the verge of redeeming himself. Then he ruined it all by committing what they saw as an act of supreme shiftlessness—he declined the headmastership.

"That would have been the ruin of the poetry in me," he told us. "I'd never have taken up my writing again. People called me lazy. Perhaps they were right. I've always been careful to *protect* this laziness."

Into his poetry Frost managed to instill the same individuality, the same avoidance of easy labels, that he maintained in his life-style. He was often invited to interpret the philosophy behind his poetry before some learned gathering. He always refused. The poem's meaning, he insisted, is as the individual reader interprets it: "It must be personal to you."

So we weren't able to pin Frost down; to say, "These are his views on prayer, on faith, on doctrine." But we can say what meeting Frost, talking with him, reading his poetry, has meant to us in the thirty years since that interview.

When we went to see him that day we were hoping, we see now, to do what journalists characteristically do: put a label on him, sum up his life's experience in words, pigeon-hole him on paper.

Robert Frost refused to be summed up. And that is precisely why this interview has affected our own faith and our approach to that of others ever since.

If he had allowed us to find a convenient category for his religion, we would have been like a man who captures a butterfly. He pins it to a board and, to his sorrow, discovers that he hasn't caught the butterfly at all. He can examine the thing that he has fixed and labeled. But his relation to it is changed. The very act of pinning it down has destroyed the vibrant aliveness that attracted him to the creature in the first place.

"You can't quantify a stirring," Frost told us. "You can't pin down the God within you." Meeting him has made us more alert to the mystery of God, and of each human personality. More tolerant of what cannot be known, and more willing to have it so.

Of course, we continue to try to clarify and define; that's a reporter's function. But the poet pointed out that there's a point beyond which the spiritual side of life must be protected, guarded in silence as an ineffable experience, not hemmed in with definitions or tested as the farmer with his pitchfork tried to do. From Robert Frost we learned that what's said in the silences is as valuable as what's said with words.

John and Elizabeth

Corrie's Things

They speak to us in silence . . . the physical possessions of those we've loved.

My hand moved, as if for reassurance, to the small round picture frame that Corrie ten Boom had given me years before, and which I keep on my bedside table. The telephone call I'd just received told me that my friend had died at ninety-one.

Corrie, heroine of the Dutch resistance during the Nazi occupation of Holland, bearer of the good news of Jesus to every corner of the world in the years that followed. Bedridden for the last few years in her California home, Corrie had long wanted to be with her Lord. So the news over the telephone was, in the truest sense, good.

And yet . . . death, from the perspective of earth, means absence. Restlessness seized me as I hung up the phone. I picked up the little picture frame and carried it downstairs to the living room—searching, as it were, for Corrie. There beside the fireplace was another object that had belonged to her, the antique brass kettle Corrie had brought us on her last visit to our home. I stooped and ran my fingers over the ornate hammered surface. Then I went into my study and took down from the wall a second picture frame, a rectangle seven inches high, six-and-a-half inches wide, of carved and gilded wood.

Objects. Physical things: two framed mementos and an old kettle. Why, when someone dies, do their physical possessions take on special meaning? It can't be the things themselves that we value in this new way. It's what these objects recall; some truth they continue to speak when a voice we love falls silent.

Three things of Corrie's. What are they saying?

The kettle talks to me about priorities. It was Corrie's sister Betsie who picked it out of a junkyard in the old Dutch city of Haarlem where the two middle-aged spinsters lived with their elderly father above their tiny watch shop. Betsie was on her way to the meat market when she caught sight of the kettle, dented and soot-encrusted, perched on a pile of old bicycle tires. She bought it with the meat money.

"Sister!" cried Corrie, when Betsie arrived home with her prize. "What are we going to do with that old thing? Look, it won't even hold water."

"It's not *meant* to hold water," said Betsie.

"Well, what's it *for*, then?"

"It's not *for* anything. Oh, Corrie, wait till I get the grime off and polish it! Can't you just see the morning sun glowing on this spout?

"And Mr. deGroot at the vegetable stand gave me a special price on potatoes," Betsie added hastily, because Corrie kept the accounts for the family and the little watch shop never took in much money. "And I got stewing meat instead of a roast—you know stew is really easier for Father to chew anyway—and I'm not hungry today. Oh, Corrie, this kettle will go on shining long after we've forgotten what we had for dinner tonight!"

And so it did, not only for Father and Betsie and Corrie,

but for hundreds who during the Nazi terror found shelter in their home. It shone for Corrie when she returned there alone from the concentration camp where Father and Betsie had died. It shone on respites at home between tireless trips to Russia, Africa, Vietnam. It shines in the firelight of our hearth today, saying: "What feeds the soul matters as much as what feeds the body."

In the rectangular frame is a piece of cloth. Yellow cloth, cut in the shape of a six-pointed star. Across the star are four black letters: JOOD, the Dutch word for "Jew." During the German occupation all Jews in Holland were required to wear such a star stitched to their clothes.

Because the ten Boom family were Christians, they honored the Jews as God's chosen people. When Hitler's extermination scheme was put into effect in Holland, the little house above the watch shop became headquarters for an underground escape route that stretched across the city and the nation.

A quarter of a century later, when I was in Holland working with Corrie on the story of those years, she took me to meet a number of the people for whom Father and Betsie had so willingly given their lives. At the home of Meyer Mossel—christened "Eusebius" by the ten Booms during days when a person's very name could invite danger—we sipped tea while he and Corrie reminisced about the secret room concealed behind a wall of her bedroom.

"You'd take your pipe with you when you ran in there, Eusie," Corrie reminded him, recalling the practice drills they'd hold against the inevitable raid by the Gestapo. "But you'd forget your ashtray, and I'd come running after you with it."

Meyer "Eusebius" Mossel set down his cup and crossed the room to a massive antique sideboard. From the bottom drawer, buried beneath a pile of table linen, he drew out a scrap of yellow cloth cut in the shape of a star.

"All these years I wondered why I saved this thing," he said. "Now I know it was to give to you, Corrie."

Corrie and I picked out the frame for Eusie's star that very afternoon. For years it hung on her wall as it hangs on mine—a symbol as bittersweet as a cross. To me that star says: "Whatever in our life is hardest to bear, love can transform into beauty."

And the little round frame that I keep by my bedside?

It holds a piece of cloth, too—ordinary white cotton, the kind underwear is made of. In fact, it *is* underwear: a fragment of the undershirt Corrie was wearing when the Gestapo raid came and she and Father and Betsie were hustled to prison.

The Jews who were in their home at the time of the raid—including Eusie with his pipe and his ashtray—got safely to the secret room. But Corrie was sentenced to solitary confinement where, as the weeks went by, idleness eroded her courage. Someone had smuggled a needle to her, but without thread, without material to sew on, what use was a needle?

Then she remembered the undershirt. By unraveling a hem she worked free a length of thread. And now: animals, houses, people's faces—what couldn't she embroider on that shirt! The design in my frame is a flower, with elegant curling petals and six leaves on a graceful stem.

You have to look closely to see the flower (the thread, of course, is the same color as the cloth). And underwear—even a dear friend's—well, it isn't the most costly of the things Corrie gave us. But it's the one that speaks most clearly, now that she's gone.

The circle of white cotton tells me that when we're feeling poorest—when we've lost a friend, when a dream has died, when we seem to have nothing left—that's when God says: "You're richer than you think."

Elizabeth

A Silence in Shanghai

Why do we go to church? For the sermon? The music? The liturgy? Or is it something else?

On Christmas Eve, this year as always, John and I will drive to our familiar St. Mark's Church with its glorious organ and banked poinsettia plants, for the midnight communion service. But we'll be thinking about another church, a church on the other side of the world, and our new Chinese friend, Dr. Li.

Dr. Li is an elderly physician who studied in the United States during the 1930s but who lives now in Shanghai. John and I met him there on a Sunday when we'd gone to seek out one of the newly reopened Chinese churches. We found the place on a street thronged with bicycles and pedestrians in green Mao jackets. The church turned out to be a red brick building with tall Gothic windows, and it was jammed with worshipers. Every pew was packed; people stood along the walls, sat in the aisles and on the windowsills.

At the close of the service we turned to the gray-haired man who had kindly made a place for us. "When did this church reopen?" we asked.

"Three months ago," Dr. Li replied in flawless English. His tone was matter-of-fact, but through his thick spectacles we caught a glimmer of tears. "It reopened," he said, "on Christmas Eve."

For the first few years after the Communist victory in 1949, he told us, churchgoing, though disapproved and discouraged, was still possible. But gradually the churches in China were closed, boarded up, or converted to warehouses. In the summer of 1959, this building too had been padlocked.

For months Dr. Li and his wife tried to grow accustomed to life without the punctuation of that weekly Sunday gathering—especially important in a land where Christians have always been a tiny minority.

Christmas Eve, 1959, was chill and drizzly; at the hospital where he worked, it was an evening shift like any other. Only in Dr. Li's thoughts, and perhaps those of the handful of other Christians on the medical staff, was there the awareness that this was the night when angels sang.

Dr. Li got back to his two-room flat around ten, but he could not settle down. At eleven he went into the bedroom intending to get undressed. Instead, he whirled suddenly and headed for the front door. Although not a word had been said, his wife followed him into the deserted street. Through the icy drizzle they walked, moving silently so as to attract no attention.

Left at the corner, across a square, right onto the avenue—both knew without saying it that they were headed for the church. There it loomed ahead, dark and shuttered, but solid too, and somehow comforting. *I really am here,* that red brick building seemed to reassure them. *I really came to earth this night, not just as a longing, but in a form you can see and touch.*

As they drew closer they became aware of other silent walkers. From every side street they came, alone and in twos and threes, converging on the avenue. Soon hundreds were standing shoulder to shoulder in the dark churchyard. New-comers took up their posts on the surrounding pavements. For over two hours they stood in the rain while Christmas came. No hymns, no sermon. Only . . . he is born! He is with us . . . in unspoken communion around the padlocked church.

For twenty years, Dr. Li told us, this was their Christmas Eve observance. No outward agreement, so far as he knew, was ever made beforehand to do so. Just, on this night, in homes all over this part of Shanghai, people silently put on their coats and came to stand here together.

And so it is that this Christmas Eve, when John and I arrive at our own St. Mark's, we won't be waiting for the communion service to begin. With the first impulse that says, "Go!"—with the first longing to share this night with others—the real communion, the undefeatable one, will have begun.

Elizabeth

Learning to Be Still

While John and I were in South America in 1968, the Methodist Church in Bolivia asked us to lead their annual two-day retreat for missionaries. We were terror-stricken. What on earth could two journalists say that would illuminate professional church workers—and for forty-eight hours?

So we hit on the idea of saying nothing. We'd make it a silent retreat.

At first, the best part of the idea seemed to be that it got us and our inexperience off the hook. On second thought we realized that it did much more than that. Thinking back over retreats we had attended, we discovered that we had forgotten the inspiring talks. What we remembered was the presence of God in the stillness.

So we held our silent retreat. By the second day, as our individual silences began to flow together, we became more than an assemblage of people bringing our diverse needs to God. We became an entity, a gathered body, to which God could speak more clearly than to any fragment of it alone.

We were all sorry when it was time to return to ordinary ways of communicating. One missionary told us, "I've worked with some of these people for many years. Yet only today as we sat together in silence did I know how much I love them."

From that time on, we've sought out such islands of quiet in anything from a two-week retreat to a snatched moment in a hectic day. Here are some of the things we're discovering as we learn . . .

"Be still and know that I am God." In the three millennia since the psalmist wrote those words, millions have affirmed that God is to be found, not in striving and clamor, but in silence.

But how do we find this essential ingredient of spiritual growth? Even in its most literal sense—the absence of noise—silence is ever harder to come by. Yearly the racket mounts: jet airplanes, power saws, all the sounds of an ever growing number of people living ever closer together in an ever-more merchandised world. Doctors testify to the damage done to minds and bodies by this mounting barrage of sound.

Antinoise legislation has begun to address the problem at a public level. Meanwhile there's a lot each of us can do to lower the decibels in our own vicinity. Much of the din around us we invite into our lives—the sounds that assault us from the TV set, the radio, the amplified guitar, the crowded restaurant. If the canteen staff throws cutlery around in the company canteen, we can bring a sandwich for lunch and find a bench in the sun. We can eliminate noise in the way we move, the way we close doors, the way we put things down. We can walk up to the person we're speaking to instead of shouting.

Even harder than creating external silence, however, is achieving . . .

Inner silence

Let thy soul walk slowly in thee,
   as a saint in heaven unshod,
for to be alone with silence
   is to be alone with God.

So wrote poet Samuel Hageman. But not everyone shares his experience. For many of us, to be alone with silence is to find ourselves alone with fantasies, distracting thoughts, fears. Silencing this "inner commotion" requires effort. Here's a way to start:

1. Identify the intruders. Most of us have developed defenses against painful insights that assail us in silence. Three common ones are "whirling" thoughts, daydreaming, and sleepiness. In order to use silence creatively we must learn to neutralize these devices. Choose a time and place when you will not be interrupted and sit in a straight chair with a pad and pencil. Now, try to empty your mind of everything but the presence of God in and around you. Ten minutes is long enough the first time. The ultimate aim is to allow God to speak to you, but in this first session the purpose is simply to identify the ways in which you shut him out. When an unbidden thought enters your mind, jot it down.

2. Now read over the list with God. When you spot an evading tactic, confess it to him. Did you catch yourself planning supper? Tell God you're using busyness to hide from him. Have trouble staying awake? This often masks fear. Give God "permission" to reveal what frightens you.

3. Put a mark beside thoughts that hurt. Did anger or fear accompany any of them? Perhaps it was a person's name, a forthcoming decision, a neglected project. This may be the subject your subconsciousness is trying to avoid—and the very one God wishes to speak to you about. The next time you experiment with silence, lift up this "hurting" topic to him: "Speak to me about this, Lord, for thy servant heareth."

Frequent silence
As you learn to tune out the static of your own thoughts,

return to silence often throughout the day. Times when silence is especially valuable are:

After prayer. You have spoken to God, listen now for his response.

Before Bible reading. Use the silence to empty your mind of preconceived ideas about the passage.

On entering church. Try to arrive at least ten minutes before the service starts. Think as you enter: "The Lord is in his holy temple; let all the earth keep silence before him" (Habakkuk 2:20).

Longer silences

Silence is cumulative in its effect; we'll never experience its true power until we have pursued it for a period of time. Five or six hours are a minimum, a full day or weekend better still. Many churches hold quiet days and guided retreats.

If such aids are not available to you, keep a quiet day on your own. It is helpful to plan ahead a series of readings, one for each hour. These might be Bible passages on a certain theme, such as forgiveness or healing. But they should not be long, and you should never interrupt a silence that is "building" on its own just to stick to a reading schedule.

Strangely enough, the greatest pitfall in a quiet day can be our very earnestness. We plunge into the day with great expectations and then grow alarmed when nothing seems to be happening. This results-orientated approach is the opposite of that receptive and undemanding openness that is the essence of silence. Our very hopes for the day create a "noise" that prevents our hearing the real word God has for us. A Lutheran retreat center in West Germany where we've often gone for refreshment provides this "Prayer for the Start of a Quiet Day":

My dear heavenly Father, I thank you that you are
giving me this day of silence. May I take, as a child,
that which comes from your hand: the experience of
your nearness, or "dryness," for you know what is
best for your child . . . I thank you that when I do
not want anything for this day except that which
you give to me . . . it will bring forth much fruit.
(*Marienschwesternschaft, Darmstadt*)

Group silence
Wonderful things happen during "silence in community." The
Quakers, who make silence the basis of their corporate worship, have discovered that far from isolating people, silence
leads to the phenomenon they call the "group mind."

Other denominations nowadays are experimenting with
up to forty-five minutes of silence as part of their regular services, often following the Bible reading. Still others are trying
a totally silent service every fourth week.

What you can expect from silence

You will know yourself better. Stripped of the sound bar-
rier behind which we all, to some extent, hide from our
thoughts, you will make discoveries about your real needs
and delights.

You will know others better. Quakers use silence not
only in worship but in conducting their affairs. When someone speaks at a business meeting, there is no rebuttal.
Instead, the others remain silent, each asking the Holy Spirit
for light on what has been said. Eventually someone else will
rise and present an alternative idea, and again the group
responds in silence. Ultimately they arrive not at one person's
proposal versus another's, but at the united "sense of the
meeting." Try that technique the next time there's disagree-

ment in your home or office. Where words can divide, silence draws together.

You will know God better. "The Father uttered one Word," wrote St. John of the Cross in the sixteenth century. "That Word is his Son, and he utters him forever in an eternal silence, and in silence must the soul hear."

Elizabeth

"God so loved the world that he gave ..."

Loving and giving: acts so intertwined that we cannot conceive of one without the other.

To love is to give. We know this from daily experience. The surprise is that it also works the other way.

At those times when love is difficult ... love for certain people, love for those who are different ... we can turn the statement around: to give is to love.

To offer our skills, our money, ourselves, to enter into God's eternal self-giving without, or in spite of, our emotions, is to discover, one miraculous day, that his compassionate heart has found a home in ours.

FOUR

God Breaks Through... As We Learn to Give

* Original for this book

Uncle Cliff's Secret

He had a sure formula for success.

The summer we visited Sherman, Texas, I spent a lot of time with my Uncle Cliff. He seemed to enjoy showing me the local sights and taking me through the family cotton-gin factory.

"You're twelve years old now?" he asked there one afternoon.

"Almost thirteen," I corrected him. And then out of the blue he said, "Want to know the secret of success in life?"

"Sure," I said, looking around at this thriving family business.

"GYA." That was all Uncle Cliff told me. Just three letters: GYA. "Think about them for a while," he said. "If you find out what those letters stand for and live by what they tell you, you'll be a success."

Well, we went home before I could wheedle out of Uncle Cliff the answer to his little riddle. And for forty years I puzzled over it. Again and again I played with words that might fit—everything from a childhood "Get Your Allowance," to a guess from early manhood, "Gold/Yachts/Airplanes," to one that occurred to me when I spotted gray hairs in the mirror, "Grow Younger Always."

I was approaching fifty when I paid my last visit to Sherman. The old factory now belonged to a conglomerate. One night I walked to the floodlit entrance, now fenced around and guarded, and fell into conversation with the night watchman. He was old enough actually to have known Uncle Cliff. And before I knew it I was telling him about the riddle.

"What were the letters?" he asked.

"GYA."

The guard looked at me. "Riddle?" he said. "That's no mystery. Everyone around here knows what that stands for— Give Yourself Away."

Give Yourself Away. And all the while I'd been thinking that Uncle Cliff was speaking of the key to material success. What he *had* said—I could hear him now—was "success in life." Give yourself away, the very essence of Jesus' teaching— getting out of yourself, doing for others. Succeeding at life.

John

The Point of Tithing

In Old Testament times, giving was not a matter of personal decision. The Law of Moses prescribed a tithe, the tenth part of the increase of fields and flocks, to be set aside for God. Is the same commandment valid today? Forty years ago we set out to explore . . .

When we spotted the tramp coming toward us we felt our usual vague embarrassment. He had a filthy overcoat and a week's growth of beard. We fixed our eyes on the pavement beyond him and walked a little faster. But our jovial and elderly companion walked right up to the chap. "A hot lunch?" we heard him say. "How much would that cost you?"

"A bowl of soup—twenty cents, Mister. Add a sandwich and it's fifty cents." (This *was* 1952!)

"All right," our friend said, "I'll make you a bargain. Here's a dollar. Buy your meal, but do something for me, will you? Give ten cents of this away to somebody else."

"What was all that about?" we asked when the beggar was out of earshot. "You don't really think he'll keep that bargain?"

"Perhaps not," our friend said. "But if he does, it could change his life. I know. I'm a tither."

Tithing, he explained, means giving 10 percent of your income to God, usually in the form of contributions to charity. As so often happens when a new idea is called to our attention, we begin to see the word everywhere. We read an article in *Time* magazine about a carpenter named Clyde Harris. Harris opened a small lumber plant in Pendleton, Oregon, and tithed his profits to his church. In 1951 he gave the entire five-million-dollar business to the church because he felt that his success was due to his tithing and other religious practices.

We came across an Associated Press article about a group of farmers in Abernathy, Texas, who had pledged one tenth of their crop to God. Each man reported a bumper harvest, more than enough to make up for what he gave away. Albert Hart, who had dedicated five of his fifty acres, reported that cotton on his tithed land grew a foot higher than on the rest of the land. The farmers explained these almost miraculous results on the basis of the biblical promise in Malachi 3:10. We looked it up: "Bring ye all the tithes into the storehouse . . . and prove me now herewith, saith the Lord of hosts, if I will not open you the windows of heaven, and pour you out a blessing, that there shall not be room enough to receive it."

Frankly, we were at a loss to explain these stories. We don't believe that God necessarily rewards good people with material success: the most Godlike men in history have been poor. And isn't the moral value of giving lost if it's done with an eye to getting back more in return?

We wrote to several religious groups for information on the subject. The idea of giving to charity, we learned, is not unique to Christianity. Muslims, for example, have a proverb: "Prayer carries us halfway to God, fasting brings us to the door of his palace, and alms gain us admission."

But it was probably Jewish genius that first recognized the principle of systematic, proportionate giving. The tithe was designed to remind the ancient Jew at regular intervals that "all things come of thee, and of thine own have we given thee" (1 Chronicles 29:14). In ancient Israel the first crops harvested and the firstborn animals were dedicated to God to underline the priority of spiritual values.

We also discovered that whether people give 10 percent, 5 percent, or 20 percent; whether they tithe to the church or to secular charities, the experience seems to change lives. Materially, among other ways. We were sent many stories of people who tithed and became rich.

John D. Rockefeller's mother persuaded him to give part of his first salary to charity. Later he tithed millions.

The founders of many successful businesses—Heinz's foods, Vick's Vaporub, Stanley Home Products, Quaker Oats—were tithers.

Mr. and Mrs. Lee W. Tysver of Fergus Falls, Minnesota, were struggling to make ends meet when they started to tithe. Within a month they noticed a difference. "Our bills seemed to get paid," they reported. After two months Mr. Tysver was offered a much better job, although other applicants seemed to him better qualified.

And when income did not actually improve, the quality of life did. One woman wrote: "Never having tithed before this year, I am continually amazed that we are enjoying the same standards necessary to the happiness and health of our family. I cannot truthfully say we "gave up" anything in order to tithe. Our lives are fuller now and our blessings too numerous to count."

There was no doubt about it, tithers liked tithing! So one Friday evening we subtracted 10 percent from our pay-checks and sent a donation to the March of Dimes. It was a worthwhile cause in itself, certainly. But to each other we admitted that we were also curious to see whether after tithing for a year, we might have more money in the bank than when we started.

At the end of six months we came very close to abandoning the whole idea. Ten percent was a big chunk out of our budget, and we found choosing a charity each week was a decision easy to let slide. Twice we let our tithe accumulate for over a month, until the total seemed like more than we could afford to give away, more than we would have spent at one time for anything else. It gave us a panicky feeling of overspending.

Unfortunately, this crisis coincided with the taxman knocking on our door for his cut. With the tithe and the tax we felt that perhaps we were being unfair to our own family.

We talked it over with a number of people. One neighbor pointed out that with a two-year-old child and a second baby on the way, our years of greatest expenditure were just ahead. "Why not wait until your children leave school and you're earning a little more?" A clergyman told us, "Nobody gives 10 percent anymore. No one can afford to. Besides, a lot of our taxes go to help others. Today the government does people's tithing for them."

This, we found, is in a sense true. Our government in America spends nine times more than all other sources combined for what used to be considered "private" charity: the handicapped, the elderly, orphans, the blind, the unemployed.

And the clergyman was right about giving patterns too. George Gallup estimated that in 1951 only 3 percent of the population of this country was tithing its income. Most people, far from giving 10 percent, barely managed to squeeze out two cents of a dollar for voluntary giving.

We would have written the whole thing off, then and there, were it not for one significant fact: the enthusiasm of tithers themselves. Not once had we heard of anyone who had actually tried tithing and then given it up.

One family wrote in their church magazine: "Like most households we are cutting all possible corners. But our weekly tithing is the one thing we wouldn't think of cutting."

A businessman told us, "There's all the difference in the world between handing over money because you have to and giving it voluntarily. When I'm making out my tax return, I hold on to every penny I legally can. But every time I can give a little more than 10 percent to my church, I do. I get a bigger kick out of giving money to a blind accordionist than out of all the taxes I've ever paid."

We decided to continue tithing for another six months. But we still wondered what these people saw in tithing that gave them so much enjoyment. Most of the tithers we got to know were not well-to-do; they were people to whom giving meant sacrifice. And most tithers do not wait, as we'd been advised to, until they're earning a good income. Depression years abounded with stories of families who tithed on almost nothing.

Furthermore, although some well-to-do people attributed their improved fortunes to tithing, most families who tithe from small incomes apparently continue to earn small incomes. It would be exciting to be able to report that as our giving increased our earnings increased, but at the end of a year of tithing our bank balance was exactly 10 percent less than it would have been.

For most people, therefore, tithing doesn't mean money in the bank. However, during the second six months of our experiment we discovered some of the things it can mean. Four things happened to us:

1. We discovered *joy in giving*. Before we started tithing we were giving spasmodically, wrenching each dollar from the budget with an anxious glance at the high chair Scotty would soon be needing. Each time the woman with her collecting tin knocked at the door was an occasion for alarm, hurried consultation, and reluctant, probably not-too-gracious, doling out of money.

But when we decided to set aside a predetermined percentage for giving, we found that we no longer thought of it in terms of the other demands on our income. We soon stopped thinking of this money as ours at all. We do hold on to the fun of deciding which cause we will give it to, among those we've always wanted to help.

(And if tithing makes it easier to give, it also makes it easier to say no! We have found that when we contribute a fair share to the charities we select, we can turn down other requests without feeling guilty.)

2. We discovered a new *joy in having money.* It is as if, by the expansive act of giving, we chase away the specter of the bottom dollar, which has worried rich men, as well as poor ones, to their graves.

Paradoxically enough, this easing of tension over money that comes with tithing appears to be what many people need to help them earn more money. We saw an article in the *Harvard Business Review* documenting the importance of inner calm in making a success in the business world. The discipline of tithing is certainly one of the most potent devices for achieving this calm.

It's also easy to see why money, which is picked in study after study as the first cause of husband-wife arguments, often ceases to be a source of friction in tithing households.

3. We developed a new *sense of control* **over our finances.** In order to find that weekly 10 percent for charity, we had to manage our budget more judiciously than before. We cut out wasteful spending habits that we hadn't previously noticed. Once we started using 10 percent of our income for truly important purposes, we approached money more thoughtfully, and the remaining 90 percent seemed to go further.

A forty-five-year-old editor who has been tithing for a number of years wrote to tell us that the first change he noticed was that the top of his desk, which had been the office eyesore, suddenly became neat and orderly. Because his personal bookkeeping had to be more systematic, he learned to be better organized in other areas.

4. Finally, and most important, we experienced a *strengthening of religious faith*. We seemed to have a firmer grasp on the idea of God and of love among men. Having invested a little money in the premise that there is more to life than material possessions, we found the idea itself more substantial.

Publisher Robert Updegraff tells about watching a father trying to pass off his fourteen-year-old son as a half-fare passenger on a train. The boy was miserable, scrunching down in the seat to look smaller, clearly getting no enjoyment from the trip. "He reminded me of some adults I know," Updegraff says. "They accept a lot but they don't give anything back. So they can't stand up straight and face the world with assurance."

This is not to say that giving away 10 percent pays one's debts to the world. Tithing is valuable as a token, a symbol of the fact that we recognize our indebtedness to God for everything we have. To put him at the center of our lives is the real point of tithing.

John and Elizabeth

The Valley of Decision

We met him in one of the bleakest places on earth. It's a place with a history, though—a history that guided him when he reached this place.

John ran a handkerchief across his face. "Is the temperature always like this?" he asked.

"Oh no," said Labib Nasir. "In the summer it gets hot."

He had invited us down to the Jordan Valley on this "cool" autumn morning to see the largest Arab refugee camp in the world. It stretched as far as we could see across the desert, row upon endless row of tiny baked mud huts set down in this salt wasteland 1,290 feet below sea level—the lowest spot on the earth's surface and surely, I thought, the bleakest.

What incentive could a person have, we asked Labib Nasir, to work in this merciless climate, surrounded by this desolation?

Fifteen years ago, he told us, he couldn't have answered that question. Back then, in the late 1940s, he'd been an ambitious young businessman who'd taken a degree in accountancy "because accountants who spoke both English and Arabic could get top-paying jobs with the big oil companies."

Oil companies, of course, do not employ accountants straight from school; Labib needed an interim job to gain experience. The one he found was the post of business secretary at the YMCA in Jerusalem.

In 1948 the Jerusalem "Y" was an enormous institution, offering Labib every kind of business challenge. It also offered him one problem for which he had not bargained. The long conflict between Jews and Arabs in Palestine was reaching its bloody climax that spring. Street fighting in Jerusalem was a daily affair, the shortage of food desperate. If the "Y" was to stay open, Labib realized, he would have to arrange food shipments from Beirut.

It seemed to him important that the "Y" should stay open. This was the one place in the city where young people could forget for a few hours whether they were Jews or Muslims. No questions about faith or race were asked of the boys who came to play in the gym or read in the library. It was a small island of brotherhood in a sea of rising hatred.

So Labib drove up to Beirut in search of food. The trip also meant a chance to see his wife who was pregnant and had gone to stay with her mother away from the violence and uncertainty of Jerusalem. The separation would only be for a short while, they reasoned. Soon Labib would leave the "Y" for a permanent position in the oil industry.

But while he was in Beirut taking the food to food wholesalers, the partition of Palestine occurred. So swift was the UN action that thousands, like Labib, were caught by surprise away from home. He rushed back to Jerusalem, but was stopped by the roll of barbed wire which now divided the city. The line that partitioned Palestine ran through Jerusalem, and the YMCA—as chance would have it—was located on the Israeli side of the line.

What was more, since Labib had been away on the day

of partition, he could no longer return. The population had been frozen on that date: Arabs living within the new state of Israel on that day were to be allowed to stay, but no others could enter. And Labib Nasir was an Arab.

At first he refused to believe that partition could last; that the split between Jew and Arab would harden into two independent nations. Meanwhile, by the autumn of 1948, one million Arab refugees had streamed into Arab Palestine.

Watching a whole family stake out an olive tree as home and hearing the wails of hungry children, Labib realized that he was lucky. His wife and new baby son were safe in Beirut. If he didn't get back to the "Y," he would simply start his "real" job search sooner than he'd intended. He got some letters off to the oil companies.

Though he'd been unable to return to his desk there, people still identified him with the YMCA. Wherever he walked in the city, they swarmed to him. "Is the 'Y' going to help us, Labib?" "Can't the 'Y' find my mother a place to stay?" At the sight of him, weary heads lifted and eyes lit up.

They didn't seem to realize there wasn't a "Y" here in Arab Jerusalem. The building, the supplies, the staff, were all on the other side of the barbed wire. Or almost all. Four other "Y" employees had been caught like Labib in Arab territory on the day of the partition.

That winter Labib Nasir received a reply from an oil company, offering him a job in Beirut at a salary ten times what he had earned at the "Y." He only had to write back accepting and then take his family into the comfortable life he had planned for them.

Before he wrote that letter, though, he took a drive down to the Jordan Valley, where some seventy thousand refugees had streamed to scratch out a living as best they could.

He wanted to see how these people—some of them personal friends—were getting on.

He found a vast camp where the Red Cross and the UN were doing what they could with food and medicine. But it was the people's eyes that told him a deeper story: they had lost hope.

It was bad enough in the adults, but in the children it was frightening. Little boys of ten and twelve were sitting motionless on the ground. Labib found himself thinking of the way the kids ran into the YMCA, shouting, pushing, laughing.

"I think if I'd seen them somewhere else, I would have worried about them, but I would have driven off and gradually forgotten to worry. But you see, it wasn't somewhere else. It was right here. . . ."

Labib squinted across the dazzling desert waste to a chain of bare, boulder-strewn mountains. One peak stood out, tall and strangely alone, brooding over the valley and the camp.

"They call it the Mount of Temptation," he told us.

Suddenly we understood. Tradition says that this is the mountain from which Satan showed Jesus "all the kingdoms of the world, and the glory of them" (Matthew 4:8). To gain the whole world, all Jesus had to do was to give Satan the answer he wanted. Jesus gave another answer, however, and Labib Nasir knew that, just for the moment, he must give another answer to his prospective employer in Beirut.

Labib returned to Jerusalem and called together the four men who had worked at the "Y." He told them of his decision to delay taking the Beirut job long enough to establish a "Y" in the valley. They bought a tent and set it up in the camp. They had no clear idea of what they could do: five men among tens of thousands. They wondered about starting a small school in the tent, teaching a few of the older boys to read and write.

When they announced the school, fifteen hundred boys turned up. Labib stood in the door of the little tent and almost gave in to despair. What could they do with this sea of kids?

In the tent was a football. Almost absentmindedly he tossed it to one of the boys standing near. A shout went up. Within a minute two hundred boys were running, dodging, chasing each other; eyes eager for the first time since Labib had arrived. With the tossing of that ball, the YMCA of Jordan was born.

YMCAs in America heard about the five men in the Jordan Valley, and the first money came in. Labib realized that now they could have their school, and once again he wrote to the company that was still holding his job, saying that he was not yet free.

When we went to see him in 1962, he had yet to take that well-paying job. Each time a need was met another one appeared. When the school was established, it was for a training shop in woodworking so that the boys could take a skill into the world beyond the camp. Then came a metal-working shop, followed by courses in plumbing, electricity, and hotel management. Finally, Labib moved his wife and child back to Jerusalem.

The influence of the YMCA in the Jordan Valley is felt today all over the Middle East. From it come educated, healthy young men, who have brought a spirit of hope to communities all over the Arab world. These are men who grew up in a refugee camp, pressurized by powerful voices to take the route of terrorism and violence. But these are men who've heard another voice as well—a voice which in this very place gave a different answer two thousand years ago: "Thou shalt worship the Lord thy God, and him only shalt thou serve."

Elizabeth

The Day the Mountain Moved

Hettie Taylor tells her story to John and Elizabeth
There's a secret to a faith that nothing can destroy.

The windshield wipers kept up their fast *flip-flip-flip* all the way up the valley into Aberfan where Michael Davies and I taught at the local primary school. "Did you ever see so much rain?" asked Michael.

"Never," I said. It seemed to me it had been raining forever.

We turned off the main road into Aberfan and drove slowly through the orderly streets of miners' homes. Pantglas School—the Welsh name means "Green Hollow" School—was on the far side of the town, up against the mountain that held the coal.

For nearly a hundred years a second mountain had been building up beside the first, as day after day, year after year, cable cars from the deep shafts below emptied their loads of coal waste. We couldn't see the towering slag heap through the rain that morning, and I was glad. Though like most Welsh people I'd lived in sight of these coal tips all my life, I still resented these black silhouettes above our green valleys.

Children were arriving as Michael and I stepped out of

the car, splashing through the black puddles that filled the streets. More than two hundred five- to eleven-year-olds attended the old red brick building with the friendly gabled roof.

"Good morning, Carol," I greeted the yellow-haired little girl who ran up to show us a shilling. Carol's dad worked the night shift at the mine, and when their paths crossed in the morning he always gave her a coin to buy a midmorning snack.

Michael and I hung our wet raincoats in the teachers' room and commiserated with the others on the weather. There were nine of us teachers at Pantglas. Margaretta Bates was wearing her copper bracelet with the raised elephants on it, which meant her rheumatism was bothering her again. She always wore the bracelet when it rained, and the rest of us gathered round to tease her for the old-fashioned belief that copper eased pain.

Margaretta, however, was not to be cowed. "If your joints ached like mine, you'd try anything. Did you ever know it to rain so long?"

"At least," Michael told her sympathetically, "it's only a half day." At lunchtime school would be closing for a week's holiday.

The bell rang. Nine o'clock. We headed for our classrooms strung along either side of the school's central hallway. My room was at the very end of the corridor next to the side entrance, in the corner of the building farthest from the mountain.

Michael's was directly across from mine, and as we walked down the hall he asked me how long a reading lesson should last. Michael was a teacher-in-training who worked constantly at improving his performance. "I spend twenty minutes," I told him. "But your children are older. They can concentrate longer."

As I stepped into my classroom, thirty-five seven-year-olds were creating bedlam. "Take your places, please."

When the room was quiet we said our morning prayers, asking God to take care of the Queen, and the men down in the mines, and us. Then I called the register.

I was about halfway down the list of names when the ventilator in the ceiling suddenly began to rattle. I looked up. There was a deafening roar and the whole room shuddered.

"Get under your desks!" I cried.

My first thought was that the roof was collapsing. The children scrambled beneath their desks while I stood staring at the ceiling. Now great jagged cracks appeared—not in the ceiling but along the inside wall, the one which ran along the corridor. Suddenly with a splintering of glass a great beam of wood came crashing through the window in the hallway door.

It was impossible, but . . . the whole school seemed to be tipping over, falling on top of our room. I raced to the windows on the other side of the room and began to strain at them, forgetting in my terror that the windows in this corner room were sealed against the wind.

Through the rain I could see Mr. Andrews, the school custodian, running toward the school from his house next door. "We can't get out!" I yelled.

Mr. Andrews peered through the streaming window, then struck it with his bare fist. Again and again he hit it, but the reinforced glass held fast. I tore across the room and clawed at the door handle beneath the protruding beam. By some miracle the door still swung on its hinges. I tugged it open a few inches against the wood poking through it, got my head into the corridor, and looked to the right.

There was nothing but darkness. The hall had simply

disappeared. To the left, however, a glimmer of light came from the side door. Leaning against our wall was the wall of Michael's room. Between this tilting wall and the outside door, a narrow triangular tunnel remained.

I pulled my head back. Though I spoke to the children, in my heart I was talking with God. "Stand up, everyone. *Lord, lead us.* Form a single line. *Dear Lord, keep the tunnel open.*"

I tugged the door open another inch. "Quickly, children. Come quietly this way. *Lord, don't let them panic. Let the outside door not be blocked.* Stay in line, children. Like a fire drill. No talking, Neil. *Thank you, Lord. The line is moving.*"

I followed the last child out. They were waiting for me in the drizzle, in two double rows as they had been taught, watching for the rest of the school to come out as they always did in drills.

But no one came.

Leaving them there I ran around the side of the school and stopped short. Where the school had been was a slowly-moving river of black coal slime, three stories high. The slag heap above us, supersaturated with rain, had simply turned to slurry. Even as I looked, the wall of muck swallowed up a row of houses below us.

Of the school itself, only the windows in this half front corner could be seen. Mr. Andrews was pulling children through the windows of Mrs. Williams' room next door to mine. From inside I could hear screams.

I ran back to my children. "Run," I said, pointing up the road away from the mountain. "Run as fast as you can and don't stop until you get home."

They took off and I dashed back around the corner to Mr. Andrews' side. He handed me a child, reached up for another. Then I took his place at the window and watched him slip and flounder over the black ooze to where the rear of the school had been. Mr. Andrews had two sons somewhere underneath.

For a while I lifted weeping and shivering children from Mrs. Williams' hands down to the ground. The last few she passed to me were strangely silent. It was a moment before I realized that they were dead.

Many people had reached the school by now: women in aprons, miners off the night shift with raincoats thrown over their pajamas. Together we waded up on to the black avalanche, digging with shovels, boards, our bare hands. Here was a child's pencil box. A notebook. One woman scrabbled in the muck on hands and knees, whispering, "Keith! Keith!" over and over.

Dr. Jones came. He had a son somewhere in there, but after a quick look turned swiftly, silently, to treating the injured. Sirens were blowing at the mine, and now the day crew began to arrive, armed with picks, ropes, and all the ghastly rescue gear of the deep shafts. Mrs. Williams and I were asked to stay on top of the coal slide to point out where the different classrooms had been.

Each time the rescuers' shovels touched something soft, a hush fell over the digging men. When they uncovered the first children they were still seated at their classroom table, holding hands, their faces in death calm, even happy. In Carol's hand the men found the shilling piece. The body of the assistant headmaster was found holding five young children in his arms.

A few times—pitifully few times—a child was found alive. The last living person was lifted from the mud at eleven o'clock. But hope refused to die. Once every half hour, all through the long day, a klaxon would sound. Everyone would stop digging, stop breathing, as we listened together, straining to hear the call for help that never came.

And now began an even more agonizing task for the four of us teachers who had come out alive. We were asked to go to the temporary mortuary in the playground shelter to identify the children, so that the parents would have to view only their own.

Up and down the rows of small forms we walked. Carol. David. Robert. At the end of a row a tall figure rested on a large table. He looked so natural that for an unreasoning moment I thought Michael Davies was only sleeping. It seemed impossible that he would never give that reading lesson.

The next days ran together in a nightmare of impressions. The bright orange earthmovers straining at the 2 million tons of sludge that had fallen on Aberfan; the *thump-thump* of helicopters overhead; the shifts of fresh miners moving in and the exhausted, blackened men moving out. Identification of the last bodies hinged on a necklace or a scrap of clothing. They brought me an object they believed was a clue. It was a copper bracelet with a row of raised elephants.

I didn't have to stay in Aberfan, of course. Didn't have to be reminded over and over. My home was in Rhymney—fortunate Rhymney—seven miles away. But in spite of myself I kept going back to Aberfan. The Queen came. There was a mass funeral: a hundred and forty-four people died in the slide, a hundred and sixteen of them children. At the funeral the people sang in Welsh, *"Jesu Cyfaill F'enaid Cu,"* ("Jesus, Lover of my Soul").

That's when I realized why I had to be in Aberfan. I needed what this bereaved village had to give. Oh, I heard people ask how God could let such a thing happen. I heard people say they could no longer believe. But I didn't hear these things from the people of Aberfan. I heard them from the visitors, the sightseers, the newspaper reporters.

In Aberfan I saw grieving parents open their homes to the visitors; use up their last scrap of food to feed the volunteers; tear their sheets to strips for bandages; stay on the scene asking what they could give, and then giving more than they were asked. I saw people who had lost their best and dearest handle their loss by turning outwards to fill the need of someone else.

And as they did, I saw their faith increase. I saw them pray together; I saw them fill the churches. I did not understand this connection between faith in God and giving to others until I heard a miner who had lost his only son in the disaster put into words what everyone in Aberfan seemed to know: "God doesn't send grief. He grieves with us."

He looked up at the enormous cross on the hillside above the graveyard, a cross formed of flowers sent from all over the world. "After all," he said softly, "it was his only Son, too. He gave that much."

Hettie Taylor

The Food Giver

"Freely ye have received," Jesus reminded his disciples: "freely give." Giving is our response to receiving. But what if our experience is one of deprivation?

I put the wheat germ back in the refrigerator, rinsed the bone meal from the blender, checked the temperature on the yogurt-maker, and hurried for the train. I had an appointment to meet the lady who had started our family on these and similar rituals, the nutritionist Adelle Davis.

I knew her only through her books, yet no close friend had ever had such a visible impact on our household arrangements. Cupboards that used to hold packet mixes, "instant" this and "three-minute" that, are almost empty, while the refrigerator bulges with whole-grain breads and organic vegetables. The sleeping pills in our medicine cabinet have been replaced with calcium-magnesium tablets; the antibiotics with jars of Vitamin C.

After sneezeless winters, tranquil nights, and energetic days, I shared with millions of other Americans a debt of gratitude to this stranger—and a sense of curiosity about what she was like in person. Especially, I wanted to know if this was the whole story for her. Were healthy food cells ends in themselves, or part of a total life picture that included the spiritual as well?

I was meeting her in the dining room of the New York hotel where she was having a late breakfast after appearing on a television program the night before. No trouble spotting her: at ten o'clock she was the only diner in the room. I saw a slender white-haired lady in her late sixties, and on the table beside half a grapefruit and a bowl of oatmeal—was it possible—a pot of coffee?

"Is that . . .?" I began when we had shaken hands, but the forbidden word died in my throat.

"Coffee?" she said. "Sure is. I know it's poison, but I like it."

With a sigh of gratitude I signaled to one of the waiters standing around the empty room.

No response. When I had tried three times to attract the man's attention, Miss Davis laid down her spoon. "Waiter!" she said, and three of them arrived at once.

If the coffee was a surprise, the trenchant, salty, rather abrasive quality of the woman was even more so. Perhaps because I kept her books in my kitchen, I had pictured her as a comfortable domestic sort, perpetually hovering over a pot of soup. Instead, I was meeting a fighter, a pioneer in what had been until very recently a thankless and lonely field. For forty years, she told me, she had battled for whole, undoctored food, against refining and processing methods which she believes rob food of much of its value.

"And it's been a losing battle. Every year more chemicals are added to our food. Every year the soil, where it all begins, is poorer. Did you see that TV drama about the world twenty years from now?"

I had. It was a "news broadcast" set in the not-too-distant future. Los Angeles freeways were clogged with cars vainly trying to flee a fatal smog level; Chicago had no drinking water.

"But do you know the scene that really got to me?" Miss Davis asked. "It was the one on the farm in Iowa, where the newscaster picked up that handful of dry, gray soil. It trickled through his fingers like sand, and he said . . ."

The forceful voice broke off. I looked up from my coffee. To my amazement tears trembled in her eyes. "He said, 'This used to be America's breadbasket.'" She dabbed furiously at her eyes with her napkin, but I had seen in that instant, beneath the gruff warrior's exterior, a heart that ached with love for the land.

"I grew up on a farm," she went on. "I remember the black soil, how it would spring back in your hand like the living thing it was. Have you ever lived on a farm?"

I said I had not, wanting to add, in the presence of her passionate concern, that I would tear out our pachysandra and put in Swiss chard that very afternoon.

"Ours was in Indiana. My sister still lives there, but I don't like going back. You can smell the chemicals in the air. I remember how cornfields used to look. Farmers prided themselves on the straightness of their rows—two-and-a-half, three feet apart. Today there's a plant every six inches. We poison the land, and then we make it produce, produce, produce. What kind of pigs and chickens can grow from corn raised like that?"

Not the kind, she believes, that can maintain health. "When I see a widow whose young husband died of a heart attack, I want to fight! When I see a child with cancer, I want to fight!"

"Is that how you got into nutrition?" I asked. "Seeing such things?"

For a moment she didn't answer. Her eyes seemed to look beyond the expanse of white tablecloths to that farm in Indiana before the First World War. "It was a less conscious thing," she said at last. "My mother suffered an irreversible stroke as she was delivering me."

She didn't die until Adelle was a year-and-a-half old, but the infant girl was taken from her and passed among aunts, friends, and housekeepers. She was the fifth girl and the one who wasn't supposed to have been conceived, the one who had killed her mother.

"I think my whole childhood was an effort to make up for what I'd done by being born. As far back as I can remember I was trying to feed people. I used to follow my four older sisters around, before I started school, pestering them to read me the recipes in the cookbook. I wanted to feed them and my father—to be the mother I had taken from them."

It was the only way she had to deal with her feelings of guilt. "In those days negative feelings were never expressed directly. Children were "sweet" or they were punished. I learned to hide anger, fear, and loneliness—and it very nearly killed me. No one can be healthy with such feelings bottled up."

Already, then, I was seeing a factor beyond nutrition in Adelle Davis's concept of wholeness—mental health was vital, too. When she and her husband, Frank Seiglinger, adopted two children, they encouraged them to express feelings. To spare the furniture she constructed a homemade punching bag of foam covered with heavy-duty muslin. "I painted on a face and a row of buttons, put a tie around his neck, and called him "Sneaky Pete." When George or Barbara got angry, Frank and I would say, 'It's all right to feel that way. Why don't you go and punch Sneaky Pete?'"

She rummaged through her bag and drew out a picture. "Here they are today." I looked into the frank open faces of two extremely handsome young adults. Had there been problems, I wondered, bringing them up according to sound nutritional principles while their friends were allowed sweets and crisps?

Actually, she said, the problem was the other way around. When she baked bread, all the neighborhood children would gather in her kitchen. Often she'd find a child she'd never laid eyes on before rummaging through their freezer for a yogurt.

She did recall one crisis. When George was three he brought home a bottle of cola from a friend's house. "I resorted to out-and-out trickery. But that's fair. These super-sweet products trick children's natural eating patterns." She put the bottle in the refrigerator "to get cold" and, when George went out to play, poured the syrupy stuff down the sink. "Then I brewed up some strong, bitter coffee and filled up the bottle again. George carried that bottle around for days, sipping bravely from time to time—and never asked for a soft drink again."

At a signal from Miss Davis the waiter brought a fresh pot of coffee, while I cast about for a way to put the question most on my mind. "What about religious training for George and Barbara?" I asked. "Would you care to talk about that?"

"But," she said, "that's what we have been talking about! How we treat our bodies reflects how we feel about God. In fact, if we neglect this side of religion, we won't have the strength or the will for the rest of it."

Adelle Davis had not always had such an all-inclusive theology. When she was a child, she recalled, God lived in the church building where the family went each Sunday. The sermons she heard there dealt with a vague and remote place called heaven (which in any case one could never be good enough to attain) and a very real and vivid region of everlasting punishment (where one was doubtless headed). But in the farms and homes of the community, its kitchens and barns and fields, this God apparently took no interest. When Adelle grew up, she stopped going to church.

"And strangely enough, that's when I began to find God." It was a long, often lonely pilgrimage, largely outside traditional routes. But with Frank's companionship on the way, she has arrived at an unshakable personal faith. "I'm so absolutely sure that life continues when the body no longer can, that I never use the words "bad news" to someone whose illness has progressed beyond what medical science and nutrition can do to help. If your body is that damaged and you can leave it, that's good news!

"But as long as we remain in these bodies, we have a job to do—and that's to develop the bit of God that's been entrusted to each of us. I think our job on this earth is to become as much like Christ as we're capable of becoming, and that means living as he did—for other people.

"But that takes strength. It takes energy. Have you ever seen someone with degenerative arthritis? He can't do anything for others—not even think about them. People who hurt, people who are tired all the time, how can they develop their bit of God? When I see someone eating an inadequate diet, I think, *There's someone with no respect for God.* To reverence him we must reverence ourselves, just as we must reverence the marvelous earth he made and the balances he established on it."

She gave a little snort of disgust at her own eloquence. "Now I've preached a sermon, and I hate sermons."

A sermon indeed, I thought, as I walked down Lexington Avenue toward my train (breathing shallowly as the air quality was awful). But the sermon I had heard was not so much what she had said as what she was. A little girl had suffered a crushing loss, her first day in this world. And she had spent her life asking that world, "What can I give you?" If God is the power bringing life from death, victory from defeat, surely I had been close to God that morning.

Elizabeth

The Johnstown Story

What do you do when times are hard?
You give a little more.

Tib bought a postcard in the giftshop at a popular spot high above Johnstown, Pennsylvania, then joined me outside. We glanced from the picture on the card to the city below us. The photo, taken a few years before, showed smoke belching from a forest of chimneys, the blast furnaces at Bethlehem Steel spitting flames into the sky. Beneath us today sprawled a silent city, its mills dark and cold.

There in ranks of hills beyond the town were the coal mines, now also idle in the 1980s. We could see the Conemaugh River winding between these hills, the source of tragic floods, most notoriously the Great Flood of 1889.

The present emergency in Johnstown had come less suddenly than the floods, but just as crippling. The newspaper beneath my arm told the story. That day's issue of the local *Tribune Democrat* reported that Johnstown had the highest unemployment rate in the nation: 22.7 percent.

And yet . . . it was another newspaper article that had prompted us to come here. A recent issue of *The Wall Street Journal* headlined some very different statistics. People were saving money in Johnstown at twice the national rate. The

giving rate was up, too. As was church attendance. The
divorce rate, though, had plunged. Crime too: Johnstown
had the second lowest crime rate among 277 metropolitan
areas.

Clearly, Johnstown was finding answers in the midst of
hard times; answers that the rest of us needed to know. So
we'd come here to find out what those answers were, not by
studying more figures, but by meeting the people.

And meet them we did. During the past week we had
met businessmen and mill hands, clergymen, doctors, and students. Almost everyone agreed on one thing: Johnstowners
like Johnstown. The economy may be down, nature may be
harsh, but, well, it's home. People don't leave, or if they do,
they come back. "My son's working in Ohio," the lady who
cleaned our hotel room told us. "But I keep his room like it
is. He won't stay out there."

Commitment to a place. Not unusual in other parts of
the world, more rare in America. We are descendants of
people who got up and moved. The national wisdom has
been "Go West"—or South, or North, but "Go!" Only
recently have we begun to question this traditional response
to hard times. With the frontier long vanished, with the West
as populous as the East, can we still find a new beginning by
moving away?

Or is the required move a spiritual one, a discovery of
strengths and resources in our own backyard? This has been
the experience of Johnstown, and it seemed to us that one
man's story sums up what the town has learned.

His name is John Sroka. He's a businessman (real estate
agent), fifty-seven years old, father of four grown children.
John Sroka was eleven years old when his own father asked
him to go down to Long's Garage and get some government
milk. That was in 1936 and times were bad in the Con-

emaugh Valley. John's dad had been a coal miner until he was injured. Since then he'd worked on and off at the mills, but as the Great Depression deepened it was mostly off. John's dad would set out at five in the morning and come home at nine in the evening, not a penny richer. All those hours he'd have waited in the hiring hall, not daring to leave for a minute lest his name be called.

"If it hadn't been for Maggie and Jossie going dry, we still might have made it," John remembers. Maggie and Jossie were the family cows and they represented not only a steady supply of milk and butter, but an attitude. Both of John's parents came from Czechoslovakia and they brought with them some important assumptions about life, the most visible of which was that you could survive hard times as long as you kept on giving. Give to your neighbors, give to your church, give to the stranger who's worse off than you are.

Since cash was scarce, the Sroka family's giving took the form of a pail of milk for a nursing mother, or a Saturday spent weeding the garden of an elderly neighbor. When John's dad was mining, he had put aside enough money to buy a house on an 80-by-120-foot plot up on the hill. Here the family of nine (six daughters and John) raised enough vegetables, chickens, pigs, and cows to survive. The family sold milk to the neighbors at ten cents a quart. "But if you didn't have the dime, you still got the milk."

Pig-butchering time was always sharing time. People walked away with blood sausage, headcheese, and whole hams, and still, somehow, there was always enough. Giving and receiving were the same thing. When it was your turn to receive, you accepted it as part of a continuous flow. No one kept accounts; it was taken for granted that when the opportunity presented itself you would repay in some fashion.

The one thing that was not part of the flow was cash. Nobody had money, and the bank wasn't interested in home-canned beans in lieu of mortgage payments. So as hard times continued year after year, John's dad cashed in his life insurance. That provided enough money to save the house, but it was all the savings the family had.

And at that point both Maggie and Jossie went dry. That was when the Srokas started talking about the government milk. If you qualified, you could get as many as six free quarts just by showing up at Long's Garage.

"Maybe we should go," said John's mother.

John's dad never said much; he listened, he considered, then he announced his decision. He listened now. At last he turned to John: "You're the one to go."

So, as soon as he finished his early morning job (selling papers to the few men still working at the wireworks down at the bottom of the hill), eleven-year-old John took his place in the slow-moving line outside Long's Garage.

"It was the worst experience of my childhood," John recalls. "The mood of those people waiting there was what got to me. The dole was final. When neighbor gave to neighbor you kept your hope. But in that milk line I knew for the first time what it was to be poor."

John carried the charity milk up the hill to his home. "You can do whatever you like to me, Dad," he told his father, "but I'm never going to stand in that line again." John's dad listened, and he considered, and no Sroka ever went back to Long's Garage.

That spring, 1936, the rains were torrential. From the dormer window of his parents' bedroom John could see the Conemaugh rising steadily. One morning when he looked out, John knew there was no point setting out with his papers. The wireworks were underwater.

When the river finally returned to its banks, the people up on the hills came down, as they always did, to help those whose homes and businesses had been flooded. John's grandfather was one of those who volunteered to dig out the six feet of mud that filled St. Columba's Church. It wasn't their own parish; the family went to St. Theresa's, nearer home. But John's grandfather was there, shoveling alongside the other men, when he had the heart attack. His death was saddening, but no one in Johnstown thought it unusual that a man had given his life helping his neighbors.

Then came the Second World War. Steel production skyrocketed and remained high in the postwar years. John Sroka spent two years in the Marines. On his return from the South Pacific he used his GI Bill to enroll at the University of Pittsburgh, sixty-five miles away by Greyhound bus, where he studied four days a week, returning home for the remaining three to support himself and his bride, Sally (a Johnstowner, naturally), by selling houses.

Eventually John opened his own office. As his real estate business grew, he did not forget the lessons of his boyhood. "We're in the giving business," he'd tell his salesmen. "Give, give, and give some more. If you give enough, the getting will take care of itself."

As the years went by, John Sroka acquired properties with this philosophy in various parts of the state. He and Sal and their growing family of three girls and a boy continued to live (naturally) in Johnstown. But John noticed that a subtle change had come over the city. It had begun with the war and the postwar boom. Church attendance was down, as was the interest in helping other people. The Society of St. Vincent de Paul, for instance, a layman's organization named after a seventeenth-century Frenchman who worked among the poor, simply closed the doors of its Johnstown chapter.

Who needed St. Vincent's? The economy was booming. Besides, if trouble did come, the government would take up the slack.

During the 1970s both John and Sal made deeper commitments of their lives to Christ. In his prayer time John began hearing a message: *Prepare for hard times ahead.* In 1980, when the government started pulling back from its social commitments, he voiced his concern to Sal.

"Things are going to be bad here in Johnstown. The next downturn in the economy is going to leave us stranded with no help from the government and—if we don't do something about it—with no help from one another either."

But what could they do?

St. Vincent de Paul. The words came to John in his car one morning. Why not reactivate this society dedicated to helping those in need? And that was the origin of "Operation Touch," a new St. Vincent de Paul project created to help people with the problems brought on by the economic recession of the eighties.

All over Johnstown, it was a time of almost mystic preparation, as similar nudges came simultaneously to many Christians. There are 140 churches in the greater Johnstown area. Even before the recession started, Methodists, Byzantine Catholics, Brethren, Lutherans, and others were at work. They set up food stores, clothes warehouses, family counselling centers, and job referral services. Johnstown was reaching into its past to find answers to problems still in the future.

Soon, as the hard times grew harder, John and Sal Sroka found they were giving more and more time to Operation Touch. To streamline their lives and help support the various projects, they sold some of their business interests.

The more Tib and I talked to people in Johnstown, the more we realized that this kind of unselfish deed was not unusual. One man, a minister, told us that he had left a thriving pastorate to open a free-of-charge youth project. "I wanted to minister to all the young people of Johnstown," Noah Martin recalled, "and I found that a church building and denominational label stood in my way."

A group of five busy doctors donate their time free of charge to those who can't pay. Mercy Hospital provides them with a rent-free suite of rooms. Local pharmacists offer prescriptions free or at cost. The *Tribune Democrat* lets the unemployed place work-wanted ads without charge. The Transit Authority has a "Bare Fare" for job seekers. On and on it goes, people standing together. People pulling together where they are, rather than moving elsewhere.

Love your neighbor as yourself. Jewish law commanded it. Jesus reaffirmed it. Here in this city along the Conemaugh we were seeing it happen.

The last day we were in Johnstown, Tib and I attended mass with John and Sal Sroka. The church was packed, which wouldn't have surprised us, except that it was eight o'clock in the morning on a weekday. Was it some special observation, we wondered? No, no, the Srokas said. It was like this most mornings.

Why do people turn out like this in Johnstown? Well, in part to offer thanks for the sense that (at least for the short term) better times may be on the horizon. But Johnstown isn't going to be fooled by that. Times are good and times are bad. In both, neighbors stick together. Church is where you go to hear Jesus say again that your neighbor is anyone who offers help, or needs it.

John

The Hostess

There's a secret to successful giving.

For a nephew's wedding in Washington, the family housed visiting relatives with various neighbors. John and I found ourselves in a pleasant blue-and-yellow bedroom a few doors up the street, where a note on the dressing table thoughtfully provided the names of the host family.

A pair of baggage racks awaited our two suitcases; the clothes closet abounded with empty hangers. Bedside tables held reading lamps, a box of Kleenex, pads and pencils, an alarm clock. A blanket left at the foot of the bed was needed at three o'clock in the morning. Everywhere in the room there was evidence of forethought, from the hair dryer on top of the guest towels to the stack of visitors' guides to Washington.

In the morning, I commented on it to our hostess: "It's as though you'd put yourself in our place."

She admitted that's just what she had done. "I sleep in the guest room from time to time. I try to experience it as someone who didn't know the house, or the city."

I try to experience it as you would. . . .

When we "give unto others," shouldn't the first step be to stand in their shoes, to see with their eyes?

Isn't that what God did for us?

Elizabeth

Becoming Better Givers

When God calls us, he calls us to be givers.

Some years ago a man who spent the day with us made everyone in our household feel vaguely condemned. There were
comments about the length of our sons' hair, about the low
state of morals in New York as compared with the part of the
country he came from.

The man is a sincere, dedicated Christian. But as his car
disappeared up the driveway, our daughter Liz sighed in
relief: "Boy, is he bad news!"

Tib and I laughed, for it was just the way we felt. Later,
though, Liz's words came back to haunt me. Bad news—but
the gospel is supposed to be good news! How much of the
time do we Christians come across as good news to those
around us? How much of the time do we register as just the
opposite, giving the message: "I'm right and you're wrong!"

I wondered how often I myself had left people sighing in
relief at my departure. Then I thought of the many scenes in
the Bible when Jesus, and later the apostles, had to fight to
keep away the crowds. How many crowds would clamor to
be close to this guest of ours? To me?

I set out to see if I could discover the difference between
the Christian who attracts and the one who repels.

If we Christians are not called to police other people's standards, what *is* our calling? For an answer, I turned to the Bible and was immediately struck by the words in God's original call to Abraham, recorded in the twelfth chapter of Genesis. "I will make of thee a great nation," God told Abraham, "and thou shalt be a blessing . . . and in thee shall all families of the earth be blessed" (vv. 2-3).

So the promise to Abraham was that his descendants—physical and spiritual—would be the carriers of *blessings* to the world.

The further I read in the Scriptures, the clearer it became to me that this promise of a people who would be blessing-bearers passed in a straight line from Abraham to Jesus, and from Jesus directly to us. Furthermore, I perceived that you and I are supposed to be channels of God's Good News in three areas: our neighbor's bank balance, his bodily health, and his spiritual health.

Material blessings

I was fascinated to see that through Abraham's descendants God brought literal material well-being to those around them. When Jacob went to live with his father-in-law, Laban prospered so much that he urged Jacob to remain with him.

Are we as individuals—you and I—today acting as channels of God's material blessing to the world?

Why not start with a list of people in our locality or our place of work who desperately need the Lord's financial blessing to fall upon them. Prosperity can come through us. Perhaps by way of a gift of money. More often in terms of practical encouragement, a suggestion, an expression of confidence.

Ask God to guide you to those people to whom he wants to pass on material blessings. Then ask him how it can best be done.

Physical health

Throughout the Bible God bestowed health and wholeness through the people who were his healing instruments. In this way Elisha cleansed Naaman of leprosy. Peter and John healed the lame beggar at the Beautiful Gate.

Have we as modern "good news people" been bringing physical blessings to those around us?

Again, why not write down the names of those we know of who are ill, and ask the Lord to use us. Remember that we are part of God's plan of blessing for these people. Perhaps it will be through sustained intercessory prayer, a special healing service, a new medical treatment we learn of, or a doctor whose name God gives us.

Spiritual blessings

Jesus invites the multitude: "Come unto me all ye that labor and are heavy laden, and I will give you rest" (Matthew 11:28).

We are good news people when we pass on to others his inward blessings of love, peace, joy, and faith. Ask him to show you which people in particular he intends to bless spiritually through you. Remember that you are not the blessing; God is the blessing. You and I are only instruments he might choose to use.

Occasionally it is possible for us to be good news in all three areas at once. A while ago this happened with a couple in the prayer group that meets weekly in our house. Norman Kramer, a former advertising executive, was one of the thousands who'd fallen victim to our recent recession. He'd been out of work for well over a year. As depression reached into the Kramers' pockets, it also reached into their spirits and even into their bodies.

Week after week Norman and Joann phoned to say they

couldn't come: one or the other of them had a cold, a fever, an upset stomach. One Wednesday night when the Kramers were once again absent, the rest of us prayed, "Lord, what can we possibly do to help?" Suddenly one of the group, Jean Nardozzi, seemed to see pass before her eyes a vision of the dining room in the Kramers' house. A feast was in progress: turkey, hot bread, salads, steaming fresh vegetables—and lots of joyous singing. It was a picture of abundance, a token of what God intended for the Kramer family.

Within five minutes we had Norman on the line. Could we all come over Friday night bringing material and spiritual blessings to live out this vision? We could and we did. It was a joyous celebration, a time of pure fun . . . and something more.

For the remarkable thing is this: from that moment on, Norman and Joann began experiencing other blessings. Norman had an idea for a new company: well-known writers would read selections from their own works onto cassettes to be sold alongside their books. As this idea began to succeed, Norman and his family began to see abundance opening up for them in all of the Good News areas—physical and spiritual as well as professional.

Seeing God as we learn to give. Seeing him transform lives and situations as we allow his blessings to flow through us to the need around us. Here's a prayer for each of us who longs to be a better giver: "Lord, I want to be fun, welcomed and welcoming, full of zest, a bringer of good things. This is the role God entrusted to Abraham's children. I would like to step into the mainstream of this calling."

John

FIVE

GOD Breaks Through... in Failure

Seeing God. Seeing him in our losses as clearly as in our gains.

Recognizing his love as surely in failure as in success. This is the discernment that lets us sing with the psalmist, in whatever extremity we find ourselves: "Even there shall thy hand lead me, and thy right hand shall hold me" (Psalm 139:10)

* original for this book

Inca Treasures

What do you say when someone fails?

For years Tib researched an historical novel, a totally new kind of writing for her. At last enough chapters were ready to show publishers—and not one was interested. What do you say to a very discouraged wife? What I said was, "Remember Donn and 'Inca Treasures'?"

Our son Donn had always wanted to be in business, working for himself. It took courage with their first child on the way, but the time came when Donn left his safe, salaried position and with his wife, Lorraine, opened a South American import shop in a suburb of Rochester, New York.

It didn't work. When Lorraine and Donn finally sold Inca Treasures, they didn't have a penny of profit to show for two years of very hard work. Tib and I went to visit them as Donn was starting the long process of sending out his resumé to potential employers. "You're supposed to put down everything you've done, Dad," Donn told me. "I can't figure out how to handle Inca Treasures."

I knew what he meant. Those two apparently wasted years would not look good on a career summary.

"I could just leave it out," he went on, "but that doesn't

seem right somehow." At last he and Lorraine decided to set down exactly what had happened.

A few months later Donn landed the excellent job he holds today, winning out over scores of other applicants. How had it come about? One day his boss explained.

"That little business you started, Don—that's what gave you the edge. We were looking for someone with a spirit of adventure. You didn't succeed, but what was important to us was that you tried."

"Maybe," I told Tib, "that's the way God looks at what we label 'failure.'"

I don't know what will come of Tib's effort to stretch her skills, to risk the new. But I think I hear God saying, "I'm glad you tried."

John

The Loser

How does a man keep going when the jeers are louder than the cheers?

Aboard the plane to Ohio I thought about the man I was traveling to meet. I knew Walter Alston only as a name in the newspapers: manager of the Los Angeles Dodgers who had just defeated the New York Yankees in the World Series, four games to nil. "Alston Genius" . . . "Alston Strategy Pays Off" . . . "Brilliant Manager's Triumphant Comeback" read the headlines of the news clippings on my lap. I wondered anxiously if he would detail his managerial decisions and force me to admit how little I understand baseball.

Because it was not the victory I was interested in. It was not this year, 1963, but the year before, that I wanted to ask about—the year the now world champions had suffered the most embarrassing defeat of their history. . . .

In 1962, with only a week of the regular season to play, the Dodgers had been way ahead of every other team. And then suddenly, unaccountably, they had started to lose. They lost every game that final week, and San Francisco beat them for the flag. Many baseball writers and fans blamed it on Alston's management. I found nothing about "genius" in those articles of a year ago; the question in those headlines was "Who Will Replace Alston?"

The manager had gone back to his home in Ohio, certain that he had lost his job. The boos of the fifty thousand people packed into Dodger Stadium for the final game were still ringing in his ears. That was what I wanted to hear about: that long winter at home. For though most of us will never manage a baseball team, all of us will know defeats. I wanted to know what Walter Alston had learned about living with it.

From the airport I drove to the little farming hamlet where the Alstons live. It rose suddenly out of the endless horizon of cornfields: a church, a shop, a few farmhouses, and the red-brick bungalow with the white fence that Mr. Alston had told me to look for.

He was standing in the doorway, a tall, spare, smiling man in his early fifties, and I found myself remembering sports writers' comments about him: how in a profession where violent language is the norm, no one had ever heard him swear. How in defeat he had taken the blame; in victory given all the credit to the players. To those who had turned on him when they supposed he would be replaced, he had shown nothing but friendship when the management remained in his hands. It seemed to me that these qualities showed in the face of the man in front of me.

He invited me in and with obvious delight showed me around the house—his grandchildren's rooms filled with furniture he had made himself, the brick fireplace his father had built, the table he had just finished in the playroom.

Obvious too was the pride he took in introducing his family. Four generations lived in the red-brick house. In her ground-floor room I met Mrs. Alston's mother and the Alstons' daughter, Doris. Upstairs in the kitchen Mrs. Alston was starting lunch. Grandchildren were in and out. I was thinking, as we went from room to room, that somewhere in this home, where four generations lived so simply and cheerfully together, lay the secret of a personality like Walter Alston.

"How do I handle defeat?" he repeated when we were seated in the living room. "Before I could answer that one I'd have to ask another. When am I defeated? In baseball you can lose one game and look terrible. Two weeks or two months later, your overall record—that game included—may be the best in the league."

Baseball, he explained, was a game of carryover scores: records kept and averaged out from game to game, season to season. A pitcher can lose a particular game but bring up his strike-out average. A manager can have a poor season but end up with a stronger team than the one he started with.

"When you play baseball, you have to average in every event, good or bad, victory or defeat. It's not a bad thing to practice in life itself."

Walter Alston said that as a boy he had dreamed of attending Miami University in nearby Oxford. But he finished school in the heart of the Depression, and there was no money for college in the family coffer. This seemed like defeat.

"But do you see that church over there?" said Mr. Alston, pointing to the steeple framed in the living room window. "The minister there passed round the hat. I'll never know how he managed it in those lean days, but he raised the money to pay for my tuition at Miami. And suddenly things were looking up again. Defeats are followed by victories: you can't tell much about either if you see them from up close. You have to look at them from the long view."

The person who taught Walter Alston the most about

the long view was his own father. From the window he showed me the white frame house next door with a barn beyond and a field where three horses grazed. "That's Dad's house there. Built every inch of it himself, even felled his own trees for the lumber."

A man in his mid-seventies was coming across the field now toward the brick house. "Dad is the happiest person I know. And yet he might have been a bitter old man—would have been if it weren't for this secret of the long view."

In the 1920s Emmons Alston did not have the money to buy a farm, but he felt he could afford to sharecrop a larger place. So he moved his family from the 100-acre site to 260 acres and bought the additional equipment and stock to go with it.

What neither Emmons Alston nor anyone else had foreseen, of course, was the coming Depression, when many of the small farmers of western Ohio were ruined. Before long the Alstons had to sell not only their new machinery and animals but their other assets as well.

Even after everything had been sold, his father still owed a lot of money. Many farmers in those hard-pressed years made use of the bankruptcy laws to cancel such debts. Not Emmons Alston. He got a job unloading steel for the Ford Motor Company in Hamilton. It paid four dollars a day. Later he got a place on a carpenter gang at Ford, and little by little he paid off the entire debt.

"He never made enough to get back into farming again. Dad stayed there at Ford for twenty-seven years—and he's a man who doesn't think he's living when he's indoors.

"But here's the real point. In all these years I've never heard a word of regret from him about moving to that bigger farm when he did. Everything would have been different without that debt to pay, but if Dad ever thinks of it, he never says so. I know other men his age who were ruined in 1930 like he was. Every conversation starts with the time they lost a game, as it were. 'If I could only have seen ahead two months . . .' They're the defeated men. They're focusing on the loss, whereas my father averaged it in and forgot it. He looked at his defeat from the long view."

I asked about faith. Did that help in achieving this long-term perspective?

Mr. Alston thought a minute, and then told this story about his grandfather. He, too, had been a defeated man by materialistic standards. He was one of those farmers who worked from morning till night every day for a lifetime and got just a little poorer each year.

"I remember harvesting corn with him in the autumn. I was twelve when I started driving the cultivator, guiding the horses round and round the field thirteen hours at a stretch. At night I'd almost be too tired to eat my supper. And yet the thing I remember best about the harvest season was Grandpa reading aloud from the Bible as I fell asleep, his eyes shining with faith and hope. I guess you could say the viewpoint he'd given himself was eternity. He wasn't going to judge whether or not he'd been defeated until he could see his record from the vantage point of the hereafter. Therefore, he kept looking forward. He kept going."

Mrs. Alston put her head around the door and told us lunch was ready. We sat around the big table in the kitchen: Mr. Alston and his wife, his father and his mother-in-law, his daughter and son-in-law, his grandson and granddaughter. We talked about the children's school, the horses, the Sunday school classes Doris and her husband teach in that same little church. And suddenly I knew what the secret of this family was. Mr. Alston had just said it: "He kept going." Wasn't that what a family was, above all—a going-on in spite of setbacks and troubles?

As I flew back home from Ohio, I realized that I'd been a witness to real success. Not success in the baseball scene, but success in living. While baseball writers were calling Mr. Alston's 1963 victory a "triumphant comeback," I saw it as a lesson in the long view. Walter Alston did not come back. In his own mind, he was never away.

Elizabeth

The Music He Couldn't Sell

He was about to encounter problems no composer before him had ever faced. Instead of working for a wealthy patron, he was going to try to write for the public.

His family hadn't wanted him to be a musician at all. At his father's insistence he'd entered the university in his home town of Halle, Germany, to study law. The seventeen-year-old's own love, though, was music. He would skip law lectures to improvise on the organ at a nearby church—so brilliantly that the church took him on as organist.

The family consoled themselves that the talented young man could pursue two careers: organ-playing *and* law.

Actually, George Frederick Handel wanted neither. He hated law, and although he loved the organ, his passion was opera. Traveling opera companies seldom came to out-of-the-way Halle, and so at eighteen Handel left his organist's job and his university classes and made his way to Italy, center of the opera world.

For several years he shuttled between one noble Italian court and another, learning from the masters, writing operas that astonished all who heard them.

Everywhere, that is, but Rome, where the Pope disapproved of stage works. And so in Rome Handel experimented with a new form: a story told in song but without costumes or action—the oratorio.

So great did Handel's reputation become during his seven years in Italy that in 1710 a German prince, George Ludwig of Hanover, offered him a position as his court musician. In those days before copyright laws, such a job was the dream of every composer. Handel's exact contemporary, Bach, held such posts all his life, none so well-paid or prestigious as the one being offered the twenty-five-year-old Handel.

True, it meant writing to the instructions of the employer, wearing a uniform, being in fact a high-grade servant. But it was the only security a musician could know, and Handel accepted.

Within months his independent spirit was chafing. He learned from those who visited the small, sleepy court at Hanover that Italian opera had recently been introduced to London. These travelers said that in London there existed something one could find nowhere else on earth: a large and prosperous merchant class—people with time for entertainment and money to spend on it.

London. Was it possible that there a composer might make his own way? Handel begged George Ludwig for a short leave of absence.

His noble master granted it with misgivings. "For a reasonable time," he cautioned his court composer.

The reasonable time stretched into fifty years.

Not that Handel intended staying so long. He lingered in London six months, then another six, turning out one melodious Italian opera after another until, still not thirty years old, he found himself the most popular composer in England. Noblemen vied to have this brilliant keyboard improviser at their parties. Queen Anne commissioned music from him for state occasions.

Above all, the "public"—that strange new phenomenon—took him to their hearts.

But the public heart, as artists ever since have learned, is infinitely fickle. London newspapers loved to ridicule Italian opera, with its gods and goddesses and farfetched plots. The public chuckled in agreement, but, for the time being, went on paying their money to hear Handel's glorious music.

The quality of his music was all the more amazing because he was composing in the thick of business pressures musicians had never faced before. Working for no master, Handel had to raise the money to mount his operas himself. He had to woo investors, rent theaters, employ and rehearse musicians, and conduct performances from the harpsichord. To lure an audience he would even throw in a harpsichord concert by himself between acts. It was a relentless schedule in a day when opera-goers expected a brand-new performance each time they attended.

Then Queen Anne died, the last of the Stuart line. Imagine Handel's consternation when George Ludwig of Hanover, whose service he had deserted and who was a distant relative of Queen Anne, arrived in London as George I of England. The story is told that Handel, fearing to show his face at court, wrote the exquisite *Water Music* and arranged to have it played on a barge as the new king was rowed up the Thames.

"What is that heavenly music!" George is said to have exclaimed. "I must meet the composer."

Handel was soon again receiving royal commissions. But the court George I headed in England was nearly as stodgy as the one in Hanover, and Handel's chief output continued to be operas for the public.

The unpredictable public. In 1728 a composer named John Gay staged a hilarious takeoff of Italian opera. *The Beggar's Opera* was an instant success, and overnight Handel was out of fashion.

For a while he fought back. But though he turned out score after splendid score; though he combed the continent for well-known singers, luring them to London with tremendous salaries, Italian opera in England was dead. At last, deep in debt, Handel admitted defeat. To pay his creditors he turned to concert giving, and found himself remembering a form he had experimented with years before in Rome.

Oratorio. A story told in music alone. No need for expensive costumes and staging. No high-priced imported stars. If he set texts in English, he could use local singers. As for the dramatic situations necessary to spark his creativity, what richer source could there be than the Bible?

It was a new kind of music—so very new, in fact, that Handel himself seems not to have grasped its true potential. Though the oratorios were well received, Handel kept returning to the outmoded medium of Baroque Italian opera, trying to boost attendance with ever more sensational stage effects: dancing bears, a mechanical dragon belching fire. One after another, his operas failed, until 1737, exhausted from overwork and disappointment, he suffered a paralyzing stroke.

With his right arm useless, he seemed to have reached the end of his performing days. Doctors sent him to the continent to take hot baths—a kindly way of telling the fifty-two-year-old man that he was fit for nothing but the life of an invalid.

All over Europe music lovers grieved. "Handel's great days are over," wrote the prince who was to become Frederick the Great of Prussia. "His inspiration is exhausted."

In fact, Handel's greatest music lay in the future.

Doctors have never satisfactorily explained Handel's near-miraculous recovery. All that is known is that one day the nuns at the rest home in Germany heard coming from the harpsichord what seemed the playing of an angel. Handel, the use of his arm unaccountably restored, was improvising ecstatic music.

He returned to London in 1738 to compose *Saul,* and *Israel in Egypt,* the most profound oratorios he had yet written. And still he did not grasp what his great contribution would be to the world of music. Once again he returned to opera, borrowing heavily in 1740 for two new productions.

Both failed on opening.

Handel had reached the low point of his career. Once again he owed immense sums of money, which somehow must be paid off. In the England of that day, men every bit as well-known as Handel could end their lives in debtors' prison.

It was at this despairing moment in the summer of 1741 that he received an invitation to write an oratorio for a charity concert to be held in Dublin the following spring. As mysterious as his recovery from an "irreversible" stroke is the fact that, at this time of his own great need, Handel should have accepted a commission that would pay almost nothing. But accept he did, setting to work on *Messiah* on August 22.

Handel had always been a prodigious worker, but in the writing of this music something more than his own immense energy seemed to take over. Removing Handel's untouched supper one evening, his servant saw tears streaming down the composer's cheeks. The music on the table before him was the "Hallelujah Chorus."

The entire enormous work was complete on September 14, only twenty-three days after he began. Handel stared at the bulky manuscript unbelievingly, as though he himself did not know where it had come from. "I think," he said at last, "that God has visited me."

Perhaps it was this awareness that prompted him to waive even the token payment the Irish sponsors had offered. As the musicians and singers rehearsed, word of the music's beauty spread through Dublin. So many tickets were sold that newspapers appealed to lady concertgoers to remove the hoops from their skirts. The audience at that first performance of *Messiah* was not disappointed. "All classes of society are touched," reported one writer. "Tears are visible on every cheek, enemies are for a time reconciled."

"The world should know," added another, "that Mr. Handel generously gave the money arising from this grand performance to be equally shared by the Society for Relieving Prisoners and the Charitable Infirmary."

With the thanks of Dublin echoing in his ears, Handel returned to London to find creditors knocking at his door. Surely the music God had given him could go now to relieve his own need? Going still further into debt, so sure was he of this music's worth, Handel hired a hall, paid choristers and instrumentalists, and advertised in the papers that *Messiah* could be heard in London on March 23, 1743.

Perhaps Londoners were miffed at being offered a work secondhand. At any rate, the churches of London united to attack the proposed concert. This foreign showman was committing sacrilege! Granted, he'd treated biblical subject matter before in these curious "oratorios" of his, but always until now out of the Old Testament. Preachers thundered from the pulpit of Westminster Abbey, asking whether people intended hearing the sacred truths of their religion mouthed from the stage of a *theater*.

In fact, the "foreign showman" was a deeply believing Christian, a churchgoer and student of the Bible all his life.

But the campaign of indignation had done its work, and the London performance of *Messiah* was a dismal failure.

Handel was not only a devout man, but—as his devotion to opera had proved—a stubborn one. Year after year he persisted in rehearsing and presenting his rejected oratorio in London. Year after year *Messiah* was boycotted.

Meanwhile he had paid off his debts with new compositions and a grueling concert schedule. And still he could not forget *Messiah*. He might be a secular composer involved in the grubby rough-and-tumble of the new commercial world, but in this music he knew that God had spoken through him.

When he had given the oratorio away, in Ireland, people had listened to it. What if he were to give it away again? Handel, childless himself, had a special love for children. He gave *Messiah* to London's Foundling Hospital. Not only a manuscript in his own hand (proudly displayed there today), but a performance conducted by him from the organ in the hospital's chapel—the first time any Handel oratorio had been heard in a church.

It was moderately well attended; enough so that Handel repeated the charity performance the following year . . . and the next. People were lured at first by the chance to hear the world's most famous organist. But as the years passed they began also to hear the music they had refused for so long to listen to.

The yearly performance became the highlight of the London season. By the age of sixty-seven the composer was blind, but every year until his death at seventy-four he continued to rehearse and conduct *Messiah* for the Foundling Hospital. As he was led by two children to the organ, the audience would weep with pity. As he began to play, they would weep with joy.

Handel was buried among other national heroes in a

grand state funeral in Westminster Abbey, the word "foreign" long forgotten. And still the popularity of *Messiah* grew. Twenty-five years after his death it was performed before thousands in the great Abbey where clergy had once fulminated against it. In the succeeding two hundred years it has been sung everywhere from the Hollywood Bowl to the church on the corner, the most universal music ever written.

For much of that time the rest of Handel's vast output was forgotten, his other oratorios rarely performed. Only *Messiah,* the music he gave away, kept his name a household word. And it led, gradually, to the rediscovery of his other works. Today even his operas are being revived, delighting audiences in the 1990s as much as they did in the 1720s.

From the point of view of a man trying to pioneer a new independent way for musicians, his greatest creation was his greatest failure. It never earned him a penny; it gave him immortality.

Elizabeth

The Upside-Down Advantage

Alex Ribeiro tells his story to John and Elizabeth
He wanted to be the best racing driver in the world.

The track was slippery that rainy morning when I arrived at
the race course in Snetterton, England. Snetterton, with its
famous S curve!

I'd arrived early to practice that curve one more time. I
was one of the few drivers who dared to take it flat out.
Throwing my car into the Russel Bend without lifting my
foot from the accelerator would save two-tenths of a second
and that could spell the difference between first and second
place.

Keyo, my Japanese mechanic, buckled me into my
safety harness and waved me away from the pit. The first
laps went smoothly as I warmed up the tires, keeping a wary
eye on that S curve with its protective clay embankment
where so many drivers before me had crashed. On the fifth
lap I went into the curve at full throttle.

The next minute I was sliding backwards down the
track. My rear end smashed into the embankment, catapult-
ing the car into the air upside-down. For an astonishing
moment, suspended in my harness, I saw black asphalt above

my head, gray sky where the pavement should have been. Then the car landed on its nose, bounced, came down again, rolled over, threw all four tires, and came to a smoking halt, right side up. My team ran across the track with fire extinguishers. When they saw me jump out of the car, all four men began to pound me on the back.

I borrowed another car and was back behind the wheel even before the repairs on mine were complete. But I couldn't get the accident out of my mind. Night and day I would feel myself once again hanging head downwards in the air . . . as though the experience had something to tell me.

But what? That accidents occur in my profession? No racing driver needs to be told that. That it was thanks to God I had walked away from it? I knew that too. I never started a race without asking his protection for myself and the other drivers.

Meanwhile I mustn't let myself brood over a near disaster. Forget the last race. Concentrate on the next one, and the next, and the one after that. That was the way to the goal I'd set for myself at the age of twelve.

In Brazil's ultramodern new capital, Brasilia, where I was brought up, a sports car meeting is held each year to celebrate the founding of the city. When I was twelve years old my surgeon father took me to see it. I will never forget the rush of hero worship as the winner was flagged in. The direction of my life was settled then and there: I was going to be a racing driver. Not only that, I was going to be the best racing driver in the world.

I didn't tell my parents about this ambition for several years. They worried enough about me as it was. I was a high-strung little kid who'd work for days on a model airplane and then smash it to splinters when it didn't look exactly like the picture on the box. My emotional outbursts had become so frequent, in fact, that a year or so before that fateful visit to the race track, my parents had sent me to live for a while with my father's sister who was a missionary among the settlers on Brazil's primitive frontier. Brasilia, they felt, was over-stimulating me. They hoped that slow-paced village life would calm me down.

It did better than that. My aunt Mirian was a devout, cheerful woman whose life was a nonstop dialogue with God. "How does God feel about it?" she'd ask when I exploded over some childish frustration. I had no idea how God felt, but somehow just asking the question could take the edge off my rage. God, after all, must have a lot of things on his mind, and the fact that my fishing line was snarled or my letter to my parents had smudged couldn't seem so very terrible to him.

I loved that frontier town with its rustic little church. Before I returned to Brasilia I went forward one Sunday morning to the rough-hewn altar and gave my life to Jesus.

Everyone noticed the change in me when I got home. I didn't get angry as often, and I no longer smashed things. Still, I didn't tell my parents about my ambition to become a racing car driver until I was seventeen. That year I asked my dad if I could have his run-down old VW beetle to turn into a racer.

Dad let me have the car with the understanding that I was not to ask for any money to pay for the work on it. For a year, four friends and I scrounged used parts from local scrap dealers and worked to modify Dad's VW. When we drove our backyard creation to the yearly race, people laughed. But the Ugly Duckling shot across the finish line in second place!

Reporters said second place was a good showing for boys still in their teens and had words of praise for me as the driver. I was on my way to my goal. With the help of auto-racing magazines, I mapped out my life. First, I would race in Brazil to attract a sponsor: it can cost thousands to air freight a car and team to races around the world, and this money is usually put up by businesses.

With a sponsor I'd climb through the various classes until I reached Formula One. There are only thirty Formula One drivers in a Grand Prix race—and fifteen thousand hopefuls vying for these thirty spots. The first six drivers to cross the finish line at a Grand Prix are awarded points, and the man with the most points at the end of the year is declared World Champion.

That's where I was heading. I started off well. I won over half my races in 1973, which according to the papers was a remarkable record. By 1974 I was already competing in the European Formula Three circuit, about halfway up the ladder to the top.

Up to that point I'd had to scramble for financial support. That year, at a race in Italy, I got a call from a Brazilian company asking me to race for them.

"For the first time, sponsors are coming to me!" I said in a long-distance phone call to my bride, Barbara, back in Brazil.

Now everything was subordinated to my drive to the top. On the road I arrived early for practice, worked late in the pit. Once a French driver whose eyes were giving him trouble and who knew that I was a Christian asked if I had time to talk.

"Sure," I said. But somehow I never found that time.

In 1976 I got an invitation to drive exclusively for a Formula One team. At last I had a shot at being world champion.

Unfortunately my first season was a bad one; 1978 and 1979 were no better. I kept getting into trouble for reasons I couldn't understand. In South Africa, coming down the end stretch at 210 mph, I hit my brakes but there were no brakes . . . I had to coast off onto the verge. At Watkins Glen, New York, the steering wheel came off in my hand and I narrowly escaped another accident. In Long Beach, California, my car threw oil all over the track and they black flagged me.

My wife and I were staying aboard the Queen Mary while I raced in Long Beach. I came in that night and slumped onto the sofa in our room.

"I didn't get a place!"

"It's the cars, Alex," Barbara insisted. Of course this was the reason I'd been giving myself, too, but the owners insisted the trouble was with my driving and terminated my contract.

Sick with disappointment, I returned home. And there a friend telephoned me.

"Alex," he said, "how would you like to drive Imola?"

How would I like it! Imola, Italy—the San Marino Grand Prix—was one of the great events on the Formula One circuit. With a different car I could at last prove that I was good. Leaving our baby daughter, Carolina, at home with my sister, Barbara and I flew to Italy.

The car was great. I made such a good impression in my first race that I was kept on to drive in the next two, the last events of the season. But in the second race, to my disgust, I didn't even qualify. It wasn't the car. I just didn't get a place.

And now here I was, facing my last chance at the last event of the year. I'll never forget the moment just before that race began. I was praying hard as I pulled my helmet on. I started the engine, rolled up to the grid. My whole career had come down to just one race. Either I did well here or I could hang up my ignition keys.

The black-and-white checkered flag fell. Sweat rolled

down my face as I accelerated. I frightened myself, I tried so hard. I pushed desperately, booting it as much as I could, braking as late as possible, recalling other races when I'd pulled a last lap win out of the dust of the cars ahead of me.

But this time it didn't happen. I watched the first six cars in front of me roar past the judges, then sputtered up to the pit and crawled out of the car. It was the end of the dream that had begun at the age of twelve.

I wanted to hide, to become invisible, but I'd been in too many TV racing events to get away with that. On the flight home people kept stopping at my seat for autographs. "Alex Ribeiro, Loser," I felt like writing.

At home I moped about. Not even Barbara's delicious *feijoada,* prepared the way I like it with extra black beans, could pull me out of my depression. Nor the obvious hero worship of the younger drivers who came to me for advice. I was a good driver, yes, but when your goal is to be the best, anything else feels like failure. The young men seemed to value my suggestions, though, and heaven knows I had plenty of time.

Which is how I came to be sitting in our living room one afternoon with a disconsolate youngster whose career seemed to have petered out in Formula Three.

As Paolo plunged into a race-by-race recital of his misfortunes, the different tracks flashed before me, the grand-stands, the straight stretches, the curves. "Oh, the final lap at Snetterton," Paolo went on, "the car ahead of me spun out just as . . ."

I never heard what happened to the spinning car. I was back at Snetterton, too, sailing through the air with the world turned upside-down. I remembered how the experience had nudged and needled me, as though it were trying to tell me something.

Was it, I suddenly wondered now, that God sometimes allows us to be turned upside-down in order to show us a different viewpoint?

His.

I recalled that other time when my perspective had so abruptly flip-flopped. When a self-centered little boy, who thought the world revolved around a model plane, told Jesus one Sunday morning: "You matter more."

"How does God feel about it?" I heard Aunt Mirian ask. Best and second best . . . winning and losing . . . were these his categories or ours? What was God's best for me, for Barbara, for the unhappy young man in front of me? Maybe God's best is in a direction we've never looked—until our world is turned upside-down. Maybe winning is a frustrated child not losing his temper. Barbara sitting up five nights in a row with a feverish child. Having time to listen to a friend.

"Paolo," I said, "let me tell you about the Snetterton Principle. . . ."

Alex Ribeiro

Report from China

The greatest failure in the history of the Christian church was the effort to evangelize China. In 1981 we visited the scene of this "wasted" effort.

The "Fasten Seat Belts" light was on, but my badly frayed strap would not fit into its metal clasp. The stewardess hurried down the aisle. From the pocket of her green Mao jacket came a pair of scissors. Deftly she snipped off half an inch of belt and slid the remainder into the buckle. A minute later the propeller-driven China Airlines plane lifted off the runway.

John and I were en route from the British island of Hong Kong into mainland China. Our assignment from *Guideposts:* to investigate a rumor. The rumor told of churches reopening in Canton, of Bibles printed in Beijing— in short, of a Christian revival sweeping the land that is home to one out of every four people on earth.

Based on what we knew of China's history, these things were impossible. For four hundred years Western missionaries had tried with little success to evangelize the Chinese. More lives, more prayer, more money had been poured into China than any spot on earth. The result in converts? Barely one percent of the population.

Since the Communist victory in 1949, moreover, even

this tiny minority had disappeared. Missionaries had been expelled, church schools and hospitals secularized, church buildings closed down. For a decade or so, reports had trickled out telling of little handfuls of Christians—older people mostly—continuing to meet in their homes. Then in the 1960s came the Cultural Revolution. Religious gatherings even at home were outlawed, Bibles seized, believers jailed. Finally, news of the Chinese church ceased altogether.

And we in the West had written the sad final chapter: Christianity in China is dead.

The wheels of the plane touched down. Passengers sprang up and began to rummage in the open overhead shelf for their belongings. Like the stewardess, all were dressed in shapeless drab-green cotton trousers and jackets—all, that is, except for a few "foreign guests." Fourteen of us, from eight Western nations, were starting a two-week tour here in Canton.

After the hubbub of Hong Kong's jet terminal, Canton's airport appeared deserted. Only one other aircraft was in sight, another old propeller model, parked with a look of permanence at the side of the runway. Inside the customs shed, immigration officials, baggage handlers, soldiers of both sexes, all wore those same cheaply made green tops and trousers, looking (to me, anyway) like a nation going about in pajamas.

Feeling conspicuous in our Western clothes, we boarded a bus for the center of town. During the drive we saw other signs of hardship: a man in a conical straw hat guiding a wooden plow behind a water buffalo; a field where twenty women bent from the waist over a row of what looked like cabbages; slow-plodding donkey carts; innumerable bicycles and few cars.

At the first set of traffic lights (a long way from the air-

port), the white-haired Danish man ahead of us turned
around in his seat. We'd become acquainted on the flight
from Hong Kong: a student here in Canton in the 1930s, he
was making his first trip back after forty-five years.

"Incredible, isn't it?" he said. "Do you notice how well-
dressed everyone is? And draft animals on all the farms! I
haven't seen a single farmer pulling a plow."

Hardship? Clearly it was a question of perspective. I
looked out of the window again and this time I saw, not a
creaking two-wheeled mule cart, but a farmer who rode on
top of his load instead of carrying it on his back. It was the
first hint that things in this ancient land are not always what
they appear to inexperienced eyes.

And nowhere are appearances more misleading than in
the church. At first John and I were only encouraged by what
we saw. Churches were reopening (about 120 nationwide by
1981). Services were packed. "The problem," one Canton
pastor told us, "is to get people to leave." His church holds
three services each Sunday, and after the first and second
ones he must plead with the congregation to vacate the pews
to make room for the hundreds of people waiting in the
street outside.

Nor are these eager crowds made up chiefly of the
elderly. The first Sunday of our China trip we were in Shanghai. By the time we'd located a church—seven are now open
in this city of 11 million—most of the seats were taken. We
were escorted, with bows, to a corner of the horseshoe-
shaped balcony, from which we could look down on the
faces. To our amazement, most were young! At least a third
of that huge congregation could not even have been born
when the last missionary departed.

And Bibles? Yes, the man beside us was holding a brand-
new one. He flipped to what, for us, would be the back of

the book and pointed to a column of Chinese characters. "Printed in Beijing," he translated.

After the service we talked with him and a score of young people who crowded around us, the first non-Chinese Christians many of them had met. We were discovering that language was no problem; in schools, farms and factories, English was being pushed as the key to the Four Modernizations of the 1980s.

We asked whether just anyone could buy a Bible. "Yes, although there'd be a wait. The 135,000 originally printed sold out at once. You put your name on a list," a young man explained, "along with your address, family members, date of your conversion, and name and address of your sponsor."

A tiny shiver ran through me. So much information on record? In a country where only a few years ago people were hauled from their homes and shot merely for possessing a Bible? Suddenly a little scene that had occurred the previous Sunday in Hong Kong made more sense. A woman had come up to me at the coffee hour following the service at the Anglican cathedral. Was I going into China? Would I deliver these Bibles to her sister in Beijing?

What could be the point, we had wondered, of sending Bibles so far, if they were really being printed in Beijing itself?

When we reached China's capital we went to see the woman's sister. Her block of flats was on the main line of Beijing's clean and efficient underground network. The sister was overjoyed at receiving Bibles for which she did not have to register. She served us green tea in cups with lids on them in a living room where, she told us, ninety people crowded to worship each Sunday. "There are hundreds of these weekly gatherings in Beijing alone."

"But now that the church buildings are reopening," we said, "why continue to meet in homes?" She looked at us in astonishment. "Attend a registered church? But those are traps!"

And so we encountered a troubling fact beneath the encouraging appearances. Although the government was permitting selected churches to reopen, many—perhaps most—Chinese Christians were boycotting them. The scars of the Cultural Revolution were too deep and too recent for them to trust the current official mood of toleration. Instead, they continued to gather in an estimated twenty-five thousand "house churches."

"For the moment, our country needs Western technology," the leader of one such group explained. "But sooner or later the door to visits like yours will close again, and the persecution will resume.

"Not," he added with the gentle smile which punctuates every conversation in China, "that persecution can stop the cause of Christ."

We were talking in the dining hall of the commune where he had spent the past eleven years as a farm laborer, although he holds a degree in dentistry from a Canadian university. In 1966, he told us, he and his wife were arrested for holding Bible studies in their home in Shanghai. Interrogation to learn the names of others in the group was so severe that his wife eventually died of her injuries, while the dentist was shipped to this remote inland farming district. Seemingly the group was destroyed, its influence eliminated, its leaders dead or dispersed.

But here is where appearances proved to be most deceiving of all.

The ex-dentist was typical of Chinese Christians before the Revolution. Westernized and educated, they lived in the coastal cities where Western traders came and Western missionaries worked.

But 80 percent of China's population is rural. How to reach the millions scattered over the vast interior had been the great unanswered question of Christian workers for four hundred years. Now the Cultural Revolution had unwittingly supplied the answer. Overnight, Christians found themselves relocated in communes and hamlets throughout the land: joyful, undefeated men and women to whom life clearly had some secret source of meaning.

And meaning, by the mid-1970s, was what most Chinese people desperately lacked. The Cultural Revolution had been repudiated by the Communist Party itself, the Gang of Four brought to trial, Mao toppled from his pedestal. In the ensuing vacuum of belief and purpose, people everywhere recalled that man or that woman in their midst whose core of faith had never wavered. The Christian was a beacon, and the confused and disillusioned made their way to him.

Not only did their numbers begin to grow, but in the bitterness of the shifting political scene, Christians—who had not betrayed their neighbors in the recurring purges, who had not lied to save themselves—found themselves sought out as leaders. Not being Party members, they were not, of course, eligible for top posts. But, like our dentist friend who three years ago had been voted production chairman of his commune, Christians now held grass-roots leadership jobs across the land.

Is there a revival in China? We believe there is. It is happening the way real revival always does: from neighbor to neighbor, worker to fellow worker.

Everything that looked, on the surface, like death, has turned out to be life. The expelling of missionaries, the closing of Western-funded schools and churches—with one stroke, an atheistic government had inadvertently removed the two greatest roadblocks to Christianity in the East. For centuries most Chinese had regarded Jesus as "the foreigners' god," and denominational divisions had marred the witness of the church. Missionaries, and all who prayed for China, knew the day must eventually come when the Chinese governed their own united church. The Communists only stepped up the timetable.

That church is now split by a division of its own. On the one hand are those who feel that obedience to the secular government is due; on the other, those who feel there can never be any common ground with Communism. The first group is represented by the throngs pressing into the newly reopened churches, the second by the probably far larger number continuing to meet anonymously in homes.

Eventually, we feel, the two must come together. Either the government will honor its announced hands-off policy in religious matters, in which case "house Christians" will gradually gather courage to worship publicly, or else active persecution will begin again, in which case those churchgoers and Bible purchasers who survive will join their brothers and sisters underground.

But the church, the indivisible body of Christ in this place, will go on. As so often in its history, persecution has only served to make it stronger. Thirty years ago the suffering of the early church was a subject taught in Bible colleges. Today there is not a Chinese Christian who does not personally know a martyr. Thirty years ago missionaries had to teach literacy before they could teach the Bible. Today—that great achievement of the Communist Revolution—all Chinese can read, and the demand for Bibles is a hundred times what it ever was.

History has two sides: man's side and, invisible for the moment, God's. We in the West forgot that when we wrote that sad ending to the story of the church in China. What looked like the end appears now to have been only the turning of a page, the start of a chapter more thrilling than any before.

Elizabeth

The Weaver

What does a holy God do with an imperfect world?

The traditional patterns—checkerboards, stripes, zigzags—
are passed from one generation to another. The bracelet
Kuulei had just completed, though, was like no other I'd
seen. I turned the woven circlet in my hands, tracing an intri-
cate sequence of diagonals, complex and beautiful.

"What an unusual design! Is it a family secret?"

Kuulei laughed and shook her head. "Sometimes," she
explained in her lilting island English, "my mind is so far
away when I weave. I make a mistake! But I do not throw
the work away. I look to see how I can fit the mistake into
the whole. In the end I have a pattern no one has made
before."

Like God, I thought. Instead of casting his imperfect cre-
ations aside, he weaves our very failures into a unique and
beautiful design for each life.

Elizabeth

SIX

GOD
Breaks
Through... As We Read
the Bible

*For the full portrait of God
we must turn to the Bible.
There he reveals himself not
just as the deity of ancient
wandering tribesmen. Not
even, solely, as the Man who
walked the earth two thousand years ago.*

*In the Bible we meet
God as he is today . . . in our
own lives at this moment.*

* adapted from *My Friend the Bible*
** adapted from *Mother's Song*

The Old Man's Promise

Can ancient writings speak to today's problems?

I felt out of place that Sunday morning as I walked up the steps of the church. Every single person except me was carrying a Bible.

It's a cultural phenomenon, I said to myself. Back home in New York, in our own Episcopal church, if you brought a Bible with you on Sunday it meant you'd been asked to read the Epistle during the communion service. But this was not an Episcopal church in New York; this was a Baptist church in West Texas. And there were Bibles everywhere.

At the door an old man noticed my predicament. I remember that he had a freshly scrubbed and sunbaked face, and that he carried two Bibles.

"Here, young fellow," he said, handing me one of his Bibles. I was gratified at the greeting, since I was well past forty at the time of that Texas visit, and what was left of my hair was turning gray.

The old man couldn't let me have his *real* Bible, the large, leather-bound, dog-eared black one. But he did hand me *The Living Bible,* for which I was grateful. Even though I had been a Christian for several years, had read the Bible from cover to cover shortly after my conversion, and had been an editor of *Guideposts* magazine for years, I still did not feel really comfortable with the Scriptures. *The Living Bible,* in its green binding, seemed enough like any other book to put me at ease.

At the close of the service, when I returned the borrowed volume, the old man stroked it affectionately: "This is where you find the answers to your problems."

That was all he said.

That afternoon, though, as I was packing for the trip home, I came across my own Bible. I took it out of my suitcase and in my mind compared the crisp pages with the much-fingered Bible the old man had carried. Why wasn't I using my Bible the way these people were? "This is where you find the answers to your problems," the old man had said. Was I missing something vital? Had these people discovered in their Bibles a resource I was not tapping? In spite of that first eager reading after my conversion, the Bible remained for me a formidable book, the province of scholars and preachers and grandmothers; a book about people who lived thousands of years ago. It just didn't occur to me that this was also a book about me.

Weeks later, at a writers' seminar, I was talking with an old friend, Jamie Buckingham, a minister who was also one of the seminar leaders. After hearing me out on some current problems, Jamie asked casually, "How close are you staying to the Word, John?"

"Do you mean the Bible? Well . . . of course I hear Scripture read each Sunday."

"That's a start. But do you read the Bible every day, by yourself?"

"No."

"Then start at once, John. Vitamins have to be replenished daily. So does rest. So does muscle tone; without exercise muscles start to deteriorate in three days.

"Spiritual health follows the same law. If you don't stay close to the Bible, you get spiritually flabby within three days. Then if a problem crops up, you'll have no spiritual power to meet it with."

Curious, I thought. Twice now I had heard this ancient book mentioned in the context of problems—actual, real-life, twentieth-century problems. It was as if the Lord was saying: "The time is here for a more brass-tacks relationship between you and me. Roll up your sleeves and get to work." He seemed to be pointing me to a new way of relating to the Bible. Not the emotional, can't-lay-it-down experience of that first reading, but a more disciplined, structured approach.

All right. I would try it. What's more, I'd be more disciplined, more structured about it than anyone. Soon the dining-room table had vanished under piles of books, loose-leaf binders, and rows of freshly sharpened pencils. There was the entire six-volume set of *Clarke's Commentary,* which analyzed the Bible sentence by sentence in quaint Victorian style. From *Guideposts* I borrowed first one tome then another of the monumental *Interpreter's Bible,* learning the difference between exegetical and expository analysis. There were Bible dictionaries and books that dissected the Bible by tracing its ancient manuscripts.

At our Wednesday night prayer group one week I found myself, with a modest clearing of the throat, offering to "do a little teaching." There wasn't any way to stop me, so I launched into a discussion of spiritual gifts in the Old and New Testaments. Halfway through my presentation one of the women in the group broke in with an experience she wanted to share. Even though it illustrated the point I was making, I resisted the interruption: The Bible was *my* province. I kept steering the discussion back to the course I had charted, until one of the men burst out laughing: "John, your ego is showing."

Which of course was precisely the problem. For me, at any rate, there was a double danger in trying to draw closer to the Bible by starting my own private Bible college. First, as my friends were swift to point out, it tended to make me proud. And second, the part of my makeup that needed building up just then was not so much my mind as my spirit. Scholarship was important, and hopefully one day I would come back to biblical analysis, but it was hardly the place to start.

So I tried a different tack. It was eleven o'clock one midweek morning, and I was seated at my desk, reading the Bible. The past few weeks I hadn't been reading *about* the Bible, I'd been reading the Bible itself, and although I sensed that this was a step in the right direction, nevertheless something was still not quite right.

How different this was, I thought, as I looked guiltily at my untouched writing projects, *from my first delighted discovery of these same pages!* My Bible reading now had a forced quality about it. I'd get up at six and make coffee, thinking about people I knew, like David Wilkerson, who spent two, three, four hours a day "in the Word." Well, if that was the way Bible reading was done, I'd do it—and more. I read and made notes and smiled benignly on Tib when she came downstairs at a reasonable hour to find the coffee thick with age.

True, getting started on my writing three hours late put a crimp in the working day, but I figured that was the price we Bible readers paid. If it created problems at the magazine God would understand, even if my boss didn't.

But this of course was shortchanging the people who counted on me. That morning I saw that I was repeating the same error I had made with my effort at scholarship. In both cases I was being competitive. That is, I was comparing myself with others. I was trying to read the Bible *the way I saw other people reading the Bible.*

Surely, though, I shouldn't stop, just because I had made mistakes? That morning I decided to do what I should have done all along. Pray. And in prayer I eventually worked out the right way—for me—to build Bible reading into my daily life. My own individual way of reading the Bible might or might not be different from other people's. The crucial thing was to find a personal pattern I could stick with.

Strangely enough, that pattern for me turned out to be preplanned readings used by thousands of others. It was in the Washington Cathedral bookshop that I saw a copy of an Episcopal church lectionary. I picked it up and immediately knew I had found my answer. Published yearly, as are similar guides by other denominations, it provides for two Bible reading sessions every day in the year. For each morning and each evening it lists a psalm, an Old Testament passage, and a New Testament passage—and of reasonable length.

Right from the start I was glad I had made this choice. I liked to think that each morning as I read the daily selections, thousands of other Christians across the world were doing the same.

The lectionary, I soon discovered, had other advantages. It was designed to follow the unfolding Christian story through its main themes, the overview complete within one year. Each season had a special emphasis. Lent dealt with our need for repentance, Easter with victory, Pentecost with service to others. Thus the lectionary gave a balance to reading:

there was less chance of singling out pet passages and ignoring others.

Interesting also was how Tib, who had shown a vast lack of enthusiasm for my earlier efforts at scholarship and marathon reading, now seemed intrigued by what I was doing. Tib is a history buff; she especially valued the ancient roots of the lectionary system with its origins in the set readings of the Jewish synagogue. One day she said, "What if I joined you?"

And this was how I stumbled upon the second secret of sustained personal Bible reading. The first secret had been to quench my original competitive urges to emulate and even outdo others in this area. The second was to make a pact with someone else to read the same passages each day. My pact was with my wife, but it could equally well have been with one of our children, or with someone in our prayer group or our church. Often Tib and I do not read the day's selections at the same time. But that's unimportant. What's important is the shared commitment.

And as Bible reading became a regular part of our daily schedule, a strange thing began to happen. It was as if these shared readings were at the same time intensely individual, so that these preselected passages seemed tailored just for our own immediate situations.

Something similar to this happened to the disciples on the road to Emmaus. "Did not our hearts burn within us while . . . He opened to us the scriptures?" (Luke 24:32, RSV). It was the same phenomenon I was experiencing: my heart burned within me as the truths I was reading became personal.

Could it be that Jesus is still opening the Scriptures to us, individually, now, as we face specific problems?

As if to encourage me in my discovery, I found this
quote on the back of a calling card:

> I am sorry for the men who do not read the Bible
> every day. I wonder why they deprive themselves of
> the strength and of the pleasure. It is one of the
> most singular books in the world, for every time you
> open it, some old text that you have read a score of
> times suddenly beams with a new meaning. There is
> no other book I know of, of which this is true.
> There is no other book that yields its meaning so
> personally, that seems to fit itself so intimately to
> the very spirit that is seeking its guidance.

The words were Woodrow Wilson's.

One day the "beam" of new meaning would illuminate
words of encouragement, on another day words of correction. It might spotlight a specific instruction or simply the
reassurance of God's love.

One morning, for instance, I faced an emergency deadl-
ine. I had to do three days' worth of work in just a few
hours, and I was panicking. That day the lectionary selections included this verse from Isaiah 41: "Fear thou not; for I
am with thee; be not dismayed; for I am thy God: I will
strengthen thee; yea, I will help thee" (v. 10). Every time during that morning when my eyes strayed to the advancing
clock, those words had the power to restore concentration.

Another day I watched a spectacular sunset only to
open the Bible to the appointed evening reading: "The heav-
ens are telling the glory of God; and the firmament proclaims
His handiwork" (Psalm 19:1, RSV).

Tib reported the same experience. On the first day of a
visit to the whaling town of Nantucket the reading opened
with Psalm 104: "Yonder is the sea, great and wide . . . There

go the ships: there is that leviathan, whom thou hast made to play therein."

Regular Bible reading can thus confirm and underline our experience. But it can do far more. It can confirm a reality *beyond* our current experience.

It was our friends the Andersons who pointed out this aspect of daily exposure to Scripture. Gordon and Judy Anderson were members of our Wednesday night prayer group until a job change took them to Maryland. The move meant selling their house here in the New York suburbs, but none of us expected that to be a problem. Their home was spacious, reasonably priced, and came complete with swimming pool. So they went ahead with the purchase of a house in Maryland, confident that their New York home would sell promptly.

But weeks went by. Then months, and the house had no buyer. "The winter season is always slow," we assured one another over the phone. But spring came and still no sale. Summer and autumn passed. Each month the burden of two mortgages was growing heavier.

The Andersons' house had been sitting unsold for thirteen months when Judy came north for a visit. To the Wednesday night group she confessed that she and Gordon were deeply puzzled about the failure of their house to sell despite their prayers and ours. "If we could look into God's heart and see why he wasn't answering, it would be so much easier."

"And yet," I said, "you've managed to stay so confident."

"Yes. But not confident that our prayers will be answered to our liking." Their confidence instead, she said, was in God's goodness. "That's where the Bible's such a lifesaver. Every day, whether we feel like it or not, we hold on to a Bible promise. That's how we spend the energy we might otherwise waste in worrying."

She cited some of the Bible verses she and Gordon used to affirm God's caring *despite the surface facts:* "All things work together for good to them that love God, to them who are the called according to his purpose" (Romans 8:28); "My God shall supply all your need according to his riches in glory by Christ Jesus" (Philippians 4:19); "Seek ye first the kingdom of God, and his righteousness; and all these things shall be added unto you" (Matthew 6:33).

"What we are doing," Judy said, summarizing, "is to let God speak for us when we can't speak for ourselves—when the facts seem to be saying something quite different."

Through the Andersons' experience and others, I eventually came to recognize two distinct categories of Scripture. One I came to think of as Manna Verses—supplied from the Bible for immediate use, like the manna that fell from heaven to feed the children of Israel in the wilderness, each day's supply sufficient for that particular day. The other I called Arsenal Verses, because they provided a source of power that could be called on again and again, in time of need.

The same verse, of course, can serve both functions. It's the way we use them that's different:

Manna Verses reflect the oddly perishable nature of our relationship with God. We need to come to him daily for a new supply of himself. We can't capture him, box him, pin him down.

Arsenal Verses, paradoxically, emphasize just the opposite. God's Word is also indestructible, everlasting. It can be stored in our hearts just as weapons can be stored in an arsenal. Manna Verses are evidence of God's moment-by-moment closeness. He is up to date on what's going on in our lives, and he tells us so by highlighting his involvement verse for each new day. Arsenal Verses are evidence of God's unchangeability, of the eternal quality of his truth.

To depend on either Manna or Arsenal Verses alone is to neglect an important part of God's provision. It was at a Marriage Encounter weekend Tib and I attended, however, that I found the best way of all to approach my daily Scripture reading. "It has always seemed to me," Father John Mihelko told us all at the final session, "that the Bible is God's love letter to us. We should read the letter twice: once for what is being said and a second time for the Person showing forth between the lines."

That night I found myself looking at the Bible with fresh eyes, not from my point of view but from God's— reflecting on the enormity of his task of making himself known to human beings. I turned to that evening's lectionary selections with nothing particular in mind, no problems, just letting him talk to me about our life together.

The psalm was the 103rd: "Bless the Lord, O my soul: and all that is within me, bless his holy name. Bless the Lord, O my soul, and forget not all his benefits . . ."

I imagined what it was like for God to hear these words said back to him by his people. "That's good. That's how I want you to feel," I imagined him saying. "You're beginning to glimpse a fraction of my total, self-giving nature."

I could see it now. Bible reading is at its best when we do it for companionship with God. God wants to speak to us about our daily concerns. He wants us to store up his Word, which he will infuse with power in time of need. But always he yearns for us to use Scripture for the highest goal of all— the enjoyment of God for himself alone.

John

The Husband of the Mother of the Bride

What can a mere man do, with a wedding coming up?

It was turning out to be a storybook wedding after all. I stood for a moment admiring our daughter in her long satin gown, a white veil falling from the flowers in her hair. Liz and Alan, her husband-of-less-than-an-hour, were moving about under the crowded yellow and white tents set up in our garden. Musicians played, while beneath a dogwood tree, Tib laughed with friends.

The reception was going just as we'd hoped. But Tib's joy, I thought, went deeper. I was watching the *after* of a before-and-after drama that grew out of the mysterious biblical concept known as "covering."

The drama began when we learned there were to be not one but two full-scale weddings in our family just three months apart.

Our son Donn's was the first. Donn's bride, Lorraine, had grown up in Peru, but at present her family was in the process of moving to a new home in Mexico. So our house—the one in which Donn had grown up—was the obvious place for both families to gather.

Which meant, in turn, that Tib was going to be largely responsible for our son's as well as our daughter's wedding. I knew right away that this was going to create a crisis. Although Tib can write a book or give a speech to a thousand people without a qualm, the thought of having two couples in for dessert sends her into a frenzy.

I offered to help, of course—in fact, I clamored to help—but soon found I was only in the way. After all, what *is* the difference between mauve and purple? Once I asked Tib why carnations were correct for men and roses for women. The patient look I got as an answer strengthened my decision to leave these important matters to the ladies.

Tib, about this time, began having a series of physical problems, such as painful oral surgery which afterwards became infected, and a thyroid inflammation with the ominous name of Hashimoto's disease. It was my neighbor Bill Henley who showed me that these things might be connected. Bill is a corporate lawyer, and when I talked to him about the logistical problems Tib's poor health was causing with the wedding preparations, I expected practical suggestions. Instead, I got some unusual advice.

Bill and I were sitting on our side porch while our wives were inside discussing punch recipes. I found myself saying with relief that I was glad I wasn't in Tib's shoes. "I've offered to do anything I can," I said, "but there's not much a mere husband can do on these occasions."

To my surprise, Bill didn't agree. He answered with a comment that set me looking into what was for me a breakthrough idea. "The husband has the most important role of all, John," Bill said. "You have to provide Tib with her covering."

Covering? Bill seemed to think I knew the term, but I didn't.

"You know," he went on, "spiritual protection for your wife. The way Boaz gave his covering to Ruth."

For the rest of the day I found myself wondering what this ancient story had to do with our very current problems. That evening I reread the biblical story of Ruth, especially the part Bill had referred to where Ruth, alone and defenseless in a foreign land, asks Boaz to protect her. Her request is conveyed symbolically. She asks Boaz to cover her with his garment, as a sign that he will take care of her.

This idea seemed hopelessly old-fashioned. I could see the need for a "covering" in Ruth's day when a woman had no legal status except through a man. But it was hard to see how a modern woman needed such shielding.

And yet Tib's eyes, ringed with shadows, showed the strain she was under. Far too often, late at night, after she'd already done a full day's work at her typewriter, I'd find her still at her desk, wrestling with the problem of where to house guests arriving from thirteen states and six foreign countries. Bill said that I had a responsibility to "cover" Tib. Clearly, a husband's protection nowadays must be largely in the realm of the spirit. And, clearly, it was time to get to work.

So, with some bewilderment, not at all sure what I was doing, I started out. For six weeks before Donn's wedding I got up half an hour early, put on coffee, and spent the time in prayer for Tib. I began by reading the Bible to see if there was any special encouragement for her in that day's passages. I asked God to remind me to pray for her during the day.

I developed visual images that helped. One morning I thought of Tib moving through the day inside a shield of clear crystal, like a delicate French clock under its glass encasement. On another day I imagined myself holding an umbrella over her, keeping her untouched amid the deluge of demands. But the image I used most often was straight from the book of Ruth. I held a cloak over Tib, giving her the ancient protection of my "covering."

Externally the pressures on Tib remained the same, and even accelerated: where should we hold the rehearsal dinner? Who is invited to the wedding breakfast? And yet it was unmistakable: Tib's eyes were losing their sleepless, harried look.

The morning of the wedding came—along with a rainstorm. We drove to church with windshield wipers flapping. Half an hour later, Mr. and Mrs. Donn Sherrill stepped out of the entrance of St. Mark's to the ringing of bells and the skirl of bagpipes. Lorraine's family came originally from Scotland, and one of her uncles had brought his pipes. One sympathetic friend even complimented us on the weather: "So Scottish!"

Had the idea of covering really worked? That afternoon our daughter Liz, whose own wedding was now just three months away, caught the yellow bouquet. Donn and Lorraine left for their honeymoon. One by one the guests returned home. And I promptly forgot everything I'd learned. Liz's wedding would be an equal success. Tib had proved herself. I could relax.

And yet . . . what was this bizarre, seemingly gratuitous series of events, so unrelated in any logical way that at first I did not see the pattern? While we were at a booksellers' convention in St. Louis, a tiny, diseased Mississippi River tick, of all things, lodged itself deep in Tib's scalp and left her bedridden with swollen and painful lymph glands. We got home to discover that a tornado—unheard of in our area—had ripped through the neighborhood damaging our house and garden.

Four weeks before the wedding, Tib had to go to the hospital for abdominal surgery. "Nothing alarming," the doctor assured me, "but it cannot wait." Her second day home, a freak flood—the worst we'd had in the twenty years we'd lived in the house—swept away slope and steps leading to the back garden where Liz and Alan's reception was to be. Water poured into our basement. It was then I came in from trying to free a clogged drain and found Tib, looking pale and exhausted, down on her hands and knees, armed with sodden towels, trying to keep rising water from the photocopier, that I suddenly woke up.

"Wait a minute!" I said aloud as I pulled Tib to her feet and took her upstairs. Tib was experiencing assault after assault, stress upon stress. And it coincided with my failure to place a daily "covering" about her. The Bible says that the husband is "the head of the wife" (Ephesians 5:23). I had resisted that idea because it seemed to put me in a position superior to Tib. But suppose the verse was talking not about honor, but responsibility?

That very day, with the rain still coming down in sheets, I picked up my role as Tib's covering, praying for her protection with all the tools I had gathered from my previous experience. Almost immediately, I saw a difference. A last-minute crisis with the caterer she handled with a single phone call. Her surgical stitches came out ahead of schedule. The external pressures did not disappear, but their ability to get at Tib's emotions did. One week before the wedding, a hurricane roared up the East Coast, burying our just-restored lawn in leaves and branches, washing away our rebuilt slope and layer of blue-stone hauled in to cover the raw soil.

"Well," said Tib, stooping to pick up a twig, "the doctor said to start exercising. . . ."

The day before the wedding arrived. Everyone in town, it seemed, wanted to telephone us with the latest weather report. It was true. A second hurricane, Frederick, was expected to reach our area tomorrow.

I looked at Tib, praying secretly for her.

And (thank you, Lord!) Tib smiled back. "We've done what we can, John," she said. "All we can do now is sit back and watch."

And, as I said, it all turned out in storybook fashion, including the clear, sunny weather. The guests cracked egg-shells filled with confetti over one another's heads, a custom Liz brought back from a study term in Guatemala. And now she and Alan were heading up the driveway, their car covered with shaving cream and crêpe paper.

I put my arm around Tib's waist and felt her sigh with sheer contentment. The kids were off to good years ahead. And so were we.

John

Signals for the Day

Suppose memorizing the Bible wasn't a chore.
Suppose it was a matter of catching God's . . .

Recently I stumbled upon a new way of putting the Bible to work in my life. The adventure began, oddly, when I found that I had remembered a telephone number.

Up until that morning I'd always thought I had a rather leaky memory. How often, for instance, I'd tried to remember a Bible passage, with no luck. That day, however, I was having lunch with a man who I hoped would help me land a contract I wanted for our publishing company. At the end of the meal he handed me a pencil. "I'd better give you my phone number," he said. "It's unlisted."

"Fine," I said, ignoring the pencil.

"Don't you want to write it down?"

"Oh, I won't forget it," I said confidently.

The man gave me his ten-digit number along with a comment about wishing he had such a good memory.

A good memory? Later I got to thinking about that remark. The telephone number had in fact been easy to remember. Why? Because it was important to me right then.

Never had I tried memorizing a verse from the Bible for

the same reason—that it could have immediate application. As a child I had tried to learn Scripture passages because a Sunday school teacher said I should. In later years I had done so with an idea that a certain verse might be helpful at some vague future date. Never because it was important here and now. And yet . . .

For some time now I'd been aware of a strange phenomenon. The Bible had an amazing way of speaking to current situations in my life. As I read it each morning, one particular verse always seemed to stand out from the page, a different verse each day, as if the passage were illuminated by a kind of spiritual spotlight. Highlighted: Pay attention to this! It happened so regularly that I began to ask others if they'd ever noticed the same thing. They had. In fact, I found this to be a common experience in Bible reading.

Could it be that those verses were in a special category? Could they be signals from God, mystically underlined because of their significance for the day ahead? If so, why not single out those verses to memorize?

So I began an experiment. Whenever a passage stood out for me in this way I would commit it to memory. Often I could see immediately why the verse was appropriate. Once, for example, I faced a project that called for more energy and boldness than I possessed. That day Mark 4:40 spoke directly to me: "And he said unto them, Why are ye so fearful? How is it that ye have no faith?"

But the verses could also speak forward into situations I had no way of anticipating. One morning the verse that was highlighted was from the Book of Hebrews: "For in that he himself hath suffered being tempted, he is able to succor them that are tempted." In keeping with the experiment I'd set myself, I memorized it, though I couldn't see the relevance to anything immediately ahead of me. That day at the office, however, I found that a supplier had made an invoice error in my favor. If I didn't call it to his attention . . . But into my mind came Hebrews 2:18. Not something or other about being tempted, but the precise wording. The temptation lost its power; I picked up the phone to correct the mistake.

Most mysterious of all were the passages that were given to me for somebody else. One morning the spotlighted verse was Revelation 22:14: "Blessed are they that do his commandments, that they may have right to the tree of life, and may enter in through the gates into the city." I simply could not imagine why that passage seemed so significant. Yet I knew that I had to memorize it.

That same day I had lunch with a young bachelor who was planning to sell his grocery business in our suburban town and go into full-time work with runaway kids in New York City. He thought the Lord had told him to make the move, yet lately nothing had gone right. No buyer had appeared for the shop, the work he had already begun with young people in the city was coming unglued. He was frustrated and baffled.

How can I describe my feeling of awe as I began to suspect that the verse I'd memorized that morning might fit my friend's situation? "Blessed are they that do his commandments, that they . . . may enter in through the gates into the city."

"Are you . . . ," I said, a little startled at my own temerity, "are you by any chance disobeying God in some area?" I hastened to explain why I was asking such a question and, of course, I had the verse verbatim to give him.

I could tell by the astonishment in my friend's eyes that those words from Revelation were exactly on target. "You couldn't have known," he whispered. Then he told me about the affair he was having with a married woman. It was a liaison he now saw he would have to break if he ever wanted to be effective in his ministry to young people. It was an exhilarating moment. The Lord had spoken to one person by giving another a verse of Scripture.

My experiences have rarely been as vivid as that one, and sometimes the verses I memorize don't apply until days or even weeks later. Nevertheless, that dramatic encounter with my friend was not unique. It works the other way around too—friends have given me verses that are amazingly apt.

Such verses cut through externals to the core of an issue. The Bible calls the Word of God "the sword of the Spirit." I'm discovering, though, that the sharpness of the sword depends on the Word being quoted verbatim. It would not have been the same at all to have said to my bachelor friend, "Well you know it says in the Bible somewhere that if we want to reach our goal we have to obey the commandments." The power of Scripture to pierce to the heart of the matter depends on the exactness of the quote.

Memorizing is the key. Your memory's no good, you say? Neither is mine—unless it's something that matters to me right now!

John

My Friend, the Old Testament

Wasn't it just a list of begats?

On a recent writing trip I unzipped the travel Bible Tib gave me many years ago, and a sheaf of pages fell out. They weren't from my constant companions, the Gospels. No, scattered before me were the book of Job and about half of Psalms. Fingered, marked, and obviously tugged from the binding with use, these were pages from my friend the Old Testament.

My friendship with these thirty-nine books began one morning long ago when I was a private detective—well, sort of a detective. The fact is Tib and I had come back to the States from Europe anticipating a difficult birth with our first child, to find that two New York newspapers had recently folded and scores of writers were looking for work. In this crisis Tib's father gave me a temporary assignment as a "shadow" for his detective agency.

The income was welcome, but I didn't enjoy sitting in a parked car watching a doorway for hours on end, or spending days in a New Jersey hotel room writing down the hour and minute each time the phone rang in the room next door.

The first day on that New Jersey case was particularly slow. The hotel window looked onto a brick wall, and I had forgotten to bring along something to read. As I grew more and more bored I began opening drawers, hoping to find anything at all to pass the time. Nothing . . . except a Gideon Bible on the metal table beside the bed.

It had been a long time since I'd been to church or opened a Bible. This one was black with red page edges. It looked anything but inviting, but since there wasn't much choice, I opened it. I almost flipped past the Old Testament because I remembered, or thought I remembered, that it contained nothing but a long series of begats and an endless list of dietary laws for the days before refrigerators.

But that morning, as I turned the first few pages, I found myself absorbed in the story of Abram in the book of Genesis. I'd never really read this man's remarkable odyssey. How incredible, it seemed to me, that a man would take his family and leave his homeland, with no idea what lay ahead, simply because he believed God had told him to do it.

Yet I learned that Abram and I had some things in common. When Abram set out on his journey, he hadn't known where he was going; I too had come to a "strange land," New York, with no idea what the future held. But Abram had an advantage over me: He stepped into his unknown bolstered by faith; he believed there was a special place waiting for him somewhere and that God would lead him to it. I felt no such assurance.

I was intrigued, and by more than the adventures the man encountered. This ancient story was acting as a mirror; in it I could see myself. Abram set out in faith. Perhaps I could do the same.

Well, shortly afterwards, with no more than a mustard seed of faith, I heard about a job at the magazine called *Guideposts*. I have been with *Guideposts* ever since, long ago becoming a believer myself and often traveling for the magazine, carrying with me the zippered Bible that Tib gave me shortly after my conversion, the one from which those pages had just fallen.

Over the years my relationship with the Old Testament has deepened. As I have become more and more familiar with it, I have shared, through its pages, my own times of joy and sadness, and appropriated its comforting words for myself.

As with any real relationship, my friendship with the Old Testament exists on many levels.

For one thing, it keeps me company. The thing that first drew me into the companionship of the Old Testament was its spellbinding stories. I'm puzzled that I could ever have thought of the Old Testament as a mere compendium of genealogies and legal codes. My childhood Sunday school somehow missed what Hollywood found here: bravery, passion—marvelous tales of ordinary men and women doing extraordinary things.

For instance, another Old Testament companion, Jacob, lied and bargained and parlayed a few sheep into a fortune. But eventually he learned such trust in God that he was given a new name, Israel, by which the Hebrew people are known to this day. And then there was retiring, tongue-tied Moses, who was chosen by God to galvanize his enslaved people into a nation of freedom fighters. Or what about quick-witted Abigail, who secretly provided David and his army with the food that her churlish husband had refused? The adventures of these very human men and women keep me turning the pages long after I ought to switch off the lights.

And then there is its beauty. The other day I heard a radio discussion concerning the books that belong in every school library. I was pleasantly surprised to learn that liberal and conservative panelists both agreed that the Bible should

be required reading. They felt that its pages, the Old Testament especially, contain the greatest concentration of superb
literature found anywhere in the world. They quoted phrases
that are part of every Westerner's heritage: "To every thing
there is a season" (Ecclesiastes 3:1); "Pride goeth before
destruction" (Proverbs 16:18); "The valley of the shadow of
the death" (Psalm 23:4).

But there is a more personal reason I seek out this particular friend: it encourages me. I am encouraged as I note how
God used weak people like me to build his kingdom. As I got to
know the Old Testament, I found that unheroic people as well
as spiritual giants played crucial roles. There were men such as
Noah, who heard God's command and obeyed; but there was
also Jonah, who heard his command and ran the other way.
There was Enoch, who walked with God in such high heavenly
places that he was received into heaven without ever experiencing death; but there was also David, whose walk was so very
earthy that it included both adultery and murder. There was
Joseph, who resisted the advances of Potiphar's wife and
became Pharaoh's second-in-command; and there was Rahab
the harlot, who protected the Israelite spies and became the
many-times great-grandmother of Jesus. The Old Testament
shows that not only strong men and women but fallible ones,
too, can fulfill God's purpose.

One day I came across a sentence in the New Testament
that captures more succinctly than anything else I've found,
the reason the Old Testament is such a true and important
friend. The passage, Hebrews 11:26-27, refers to Moses:
"Esteeming the reproach of Christ greater riches than the
treasures in Egypt," the writer says, ". . . he endured, as seeing him who is invisible."

What an extraordinary statement! Moses was acting out
of faith in Christ fifteen centuries *before* the birth of Jesus.

He saw what would not be visible on earth, heard what would not be audible to physical ears, till hundreds of years in the future.

And this, I think, is the secret of the ultimate importance of the Old Testament to struggling Christians today. The Old Testament points to Jesus—every book, every incident. Jesus himself quoted from it regularly and observed that these Scriptures "testify of me" (John 5:39).

In them God revealed himself—his unconditional love and his unchanging character—to people who repeatedly disobeyed his law and rejected his love. Yet he held out to them forgiveness and a Deliverer. The trials those people faced had a purpose, preparing them for the as-yet-unseen Messiah. Our trials, too, are leading us to him, whether we perceive him at a given moment or not.

In the Old Testament I recognize men and women who are expecting the Messiah to come into their present situation, and from them I learn to do the same, expecting him to come into my temptations or my illnesses or my relationships.

The seemingly random events of our lives are leading us somewhere. In the Old Testament the very recognizable characters were heading toward the Messiah in the same way I am heading toward him today. They were taken out of their distress by faith, and I will be too.

This collection of books we call the Old Testament is such a rich blend of exciting stories of encouragement and hope, such a portrait of God's love for his people, that I wonder now how I got along before I made its acquaintance.

Proverbs 18:24 says, "There is a friend that sticketh closer than a brother." To me, that is an excellent description of my friend, the Old Testament.

John

Digging Deeper into the Bible

"The real treasure," the old miner told us, "lies beneath the surface."

It's a wonder I heard the collect at all. My mind was wandering that November Sunday morning. Tib and I were on a story assignment in the Colorado Rockies, and through the window of the country church the mountains were wonderfully brilliant. When I wasn't admiring them I was fretting over our company's balance sheet, and over a suspicious growth on my cheek, and over whether or not our daughter and her husband could get the mortgage they needed. In other words, it was a typical week filled with typical concerns.

So the familiar words of the collect almost passed me by. A "collect" is an ancient liturgical prayer designed to collect the scattered thoughts of the congregation and focus them on some aspect of faith. That Sunday the subject was the Bible:

> Blessed Lord, who has caused all holy Scriptures to be written for our learning: Grant that we may in such wise hear them, read, mark, learn, and inwardly digest them; that, by patience and comfort of thy holy Word, we may embrace and ever hold

fast the blessed hope of everlasting life, which thou
hast given us in our Savior Jesus Christ.

I'd heard the same words year after year on this same
November Sunday, and I settled back to hear the usual bene-
fits-of-Bible-reading sermon. In the pulpit that morning, however, was not the pastor but a layman, a shriveled old fellow
who introduced himself as a miner, long retired, who used to
dig for silver in these very hills. He spoke without notes on
the morning's theme. *Here comes the yearly exhortation to
daily Bible reading,* I said to myself.

Well . . . I sat back comfortably. This was probably the
one Sunday in the year when, instead of feeling pinned to the
wall, I allowed myself a sigh of self-satisfaction. Because I
did read my Bible daily—twice a day, in fact. A psalm, an
Old Testament passage and a New Testament passage each
morning and evening, following the selections in the Episcopal church lectionary.

But I was wrong about the old miner's message. He
spoke not about the frequency of Bible reading, but the pace.
He stressed just one word from the collect, "patience."

"I've learned," he said, his joy-filled eyes peering over
undersized glasses, "that the Bible doesn't give up its riches
to people who read it too quickly. Might reach a surface
vein, but the real mother lode lies deep. What's needed is
slow, patient digging. Just a few verses a week."

A few verses a week? How could anyone spend seven
days on a single passage? Like most of us these days I was a
busy person; my Bible reading was as accomplishment-ori-
ented and efficient as my other activities.

Back home in New York, however, the old miner's
words stuck in my mind. One morning I took *The Book of
Common Prayer* from the bookshelf and looked again at that
collect. These old prayers are honed and tightened over the

centuries until they contain not a wasted word. So, why did this one string out that sequence of five injunctions? Hear! Read! Mark! Learn! Inwardly digest! It sounded almost like a repetition of the same thing five times, but collects don't do that. I began to wonder if in them I had inherited a miniature treasure map for digging out the hidden riches of the Bible.

Suppose, instead of getting through all the appointed readings this coming week, I chose just one passage—say the Gospel selection to be read in church next Sunday—and concentrated for seven days on those few verses? The following Sunday's Gospel reading, as it turned out, was only thirteen verses long, Matthew 21:1-13, the account of Jesus' triumphal entry into Jerusalem. I decided to approach it through the five steps of the collect.

Hear!

The first morning in this process of digging deeper, I wondered if we could be missing something in not hearing Scripture, as well as reading it, as part of our daily spiritual diet. Perhaps there is a real difference between what reaches us through the eyes and what enters through the ears. When we children were small, my father used to read the Bible aloud in the evening to Mother, my sister, and me. I wriggled and couldn't wait for the session to be over, but today I know that something important was happening. Hearing is a group experience, even if the group is only two people. Hearing involves an element of sharing: someone has to care enough to read to someone else. And there is a subtle sponsorship involved: when he read those Scriptures to us each evening, Dad was saying something about the central place of the Bible in his life.

As it happened, Dad lost his eyesight in his early fifties. Yet he went on to reach the height of his career after this. I used to admire the way he would sit by the hour with his Talking

Books listening to Alexander Scourby's resonant voice reading the Bible. Dad's faith was never stronger. "Faith comes by hearing," says St. Paul. Was there a connection?

So for this week's experiment I decided to be literal. I found the Matthew selection in a cassette recording and played it frequently over the car stereo. At suppertime, Tib and I took turns reading the passage aloud to each other. The experience, sure enough, imprinted the words in my consciousness at an altogether different level.

Read!

I was a little more familiar with this injunction because my Bible study up till now had consisted mostly of silent reading. But it was new to me to pore over the same passage repeatedly. Each morning, with a fire going down in my office, I followed the story of Jesus' entry into Jerusalem. For variety I switched from one version to another, the King James, the NIV, the RSV, the Phillips, *The Living Bible*. I even dusted off my French and Italian and read the account in those languages.

Reading silently was a very different experience from hearing the same words read by someone else. Hearing was rich in overtones of connectedness and community; reading to myself was intimate, almost as if the passage were addressed to me personally. My eye would stop on a phrase or on a single word. I lingered, treasured, savored. One morning I spent the whole session on a single sentence: "The disciples went and did as Jesus had instructed them." Strangely, where at first I'd wondered how I'd ever stay with thirteen verses for a whole week, I soon found that I couldn't possibly do justice to that many verses in just one sitting.

Mark!

Mark had always meant to me "pay attention." But as I

experimented with taking literally the five verbs of the collect, I began physically to mark up my Bible. I used a high-
lighter, a specially inked felt-tip pen that overscores type
without obliterating it, choosing different colors for different
emphases: yellow for places where I wanted to praise God,
red for verses where he seemed to be giving me correction,
green for encouragement.

Straight away, however, I discovered that this page of
my Bible was getting over-inked! And the same words might
say one thing to me one morning, something else the next.
Each day, it seemed, the passage spoke afresh. So I went to
the public library and reproduced that page from Matthew. I
made a copy for each day, then highlighted at will. Looking
back over the copies I discovered that I had a record of the
week's spiritual experience.

Learn!
I'd long had a memory system for Bible verses, amassing a
personal "arsenal" of Scriptures that I could summon to
mind at need, carrying a few of them always on cards in my
shirt pocket for review.

Now I wondered if, like *mark, learn,* too, could be
taken literally. I set out to learn all I could about the passage
I'd been reading. How much did I really know about Matthew? And about Jerusalem? About the temple? About the
prophetic foretellings of this event? In the church library I
located a book delving into the original Greek words of the
account, learning how different English equivalents enrich
the meaning. Obviously in a week I could not even scratch
the surface of all there was to learn about these few verses.

Inwardly digest!
When you digest food it becomes part of your blood, cells,

and tissue. It becomes part of you. That is what I found happening with this new kind of Bible reading. In a notebook I began to jot down the number of times during that week when insights from that passage became part and parcel of the day's events. How often that happened! Verses would come welling up from inside me to illuminate or interpret or put into context the flesh-and-blood situation around me. That very week Tib and I had an overnight guest from Chicago who'd gone through a traumatic rejection by the company at the Merchandise Mart where she'd worked for over twenty years. From being their top producer she'd suddenly found herself out in the cold with not even an acknowledgment of her contribution through the years. How I could relate to her, walking as I was with Jesus through the cheering crowds who were so soon and so savagely to turn against him!

And so . . . the week was over. One Bible passage had begun to move from my head into my heart.

Once again Tib and I were in church. The lay reader walked to the chancel steps and read aloud the selection from Matthew. Once again, the familiar words. But now they had the power of seven days of hearing and reading them over and over again. With them was the memory of the highlighted portions that had leapt out for me. The memory of those verses becoming, as it were, incarnate, infused with meaning for everyday life.

I asked myself what the chief difference was in the two approaches to the Bible, a few verses intensely studied, or many chapters covered more quickly. Both have value. Rapid reading was like our drive through the Rockies, where we enjoyed the panorama in a sweep and grasped a whole topography. The patient study was like mining: digging deep to uncover riches beneath the surface.

Another week was starting. Tomorrow I'd be getting the biopsy report. I would know, too, the results of a business negotiation. And we would learn how our daughter Liz had fared with the bank. A typical week, in other words, but with something added. Another way to explore the Book where God has stored wisdom for whatever lies ahead.

John

How to Find It in the Bible

Where in those hundreds of pages was the verse I wanted?

Twenty years ago a car salesman sold me a "lemon." First he lied to me, then he refused to listen to my complaints. I was mad, of course. Everytime I chugged past his showroom, I imagined an elaborate plot in which I put the man right out of business. The anger wouldn't go away and neither would the painful knot in my stomach, until at last it became clear that dwelling on this injustice was only compounding the damage.

At that point a Bible verse ran through my mind.

Or almost did.

And that's where the trouble lay. I was a new Christian, not all that familiar with Scripture. The verse I vaguely remembered said something like, "Don't sin when you get angry," suggesting that there was a legitimate place for anger, but that it could cross a borderline where it became sin.

How could I find that verse? I flicked not very hopefully through my Bible, scanning the columns for the word *anger*. I did spot it in a few places, such as Psalm 30: "His anger endureth but a moment." But none was the quote I wanted.

The next Sunday after church I stepped into the office of our pastor, Marc Hall, and asked him if he knew the verse.

"Be angry and sin not," said Marc. "But let's look it up to be sure."

Marc reached across his desk toward three dog-eared books—a Bible, a dictionary, and one other volume—that were obviously daily reference tools. I assumed that he was going to pick up the Bible but instead he chose the well-worn third book. He opened it and ran his finger down a column.

"Let's see . . . *anger* . . . *angry* . . . here. 'Be ye angry, and sin not,' Ephesians 4:26." Marc swung the book around for me to see.

I was dazzled. Obviously someone had gone through the entire Bible alphabetizing key words, along with chapter and verse.

"What a marvelous book," I said.

"The concordance?" said Marc. "Wouldn't be without it. If you're interested, we have the three classic versions in the church library."

The three classics, it turned out, were *Cruden's,* compiled by a Scottish bookseller in 1737; *Young's,* which came along 142 years later; and *Strong's,* the most recent of the three, compiled here in America. Today various editions of these works, full-length and abridged, as well as still newer compilations, are available in bookshops and libraries.

It was exhilarating, that afternoon, tracing what God had to say about the subject that interested me at the moment: anger. The Bible passages to which the concordance steered me helped me put to rest at last the emotions stirred up by that dishonest salesman. (The references instructed me to release him from my judgment, and repent of my own sin of harbored resentment.) But a still better thing came out of that afternoon. It marked the beginning of the love affair I've had ever since with a good concordance.

I soon found that a simple alphabetical listing of key

words—indispensable though this is—is not all that such a guidebook can offer. Many concordances include, in addition, a topical index.

Once, for example, when Tib and I faced a tough financial decision, I thought I'd see what the Bible had to say on the subject of money. Under "money" the key-word index guided me to a number of helpful references, but the topical index helped me range through parallel ideas such as coins, silver, gold, shekel, mammon, riches, provision, supply.

Over the years I have become convinced that concordances are essential road maps for the exploration of the Bible. Tib and I started out using them to help us locate a quotation or check an exact wording. Now, however, we also use our concordance as a sort of personalized devotional, helping us follow great concepts through the Bible.

When, for example, our children began to think about career choices, we spent days going through the Bible tracing what God has to say about work. We also use the concordance for intercession. When asked to pray about a given problem, we go there to find guidelines based on the Word of God. What does the Bible have to say about illness, family conflicts, and decision making?

When our daughter Liz was small, she used to call the concordance "that book with the funny name." It's an odd name, all right, but a daily companion I wouldn't be without.

John

The Leave-Taking

John's mother was in a coma. What was the mystic communication through words of Scripture?

I swung my rental car into the parking lot of the nursing home just outside Louisville, Kentucky. The news that had been waiting my return from a brief trip overseas was not good. My eighty-three-year-old mother had pneumonia.

On the first floor of two-story Westminster Terrace I turned right, toward the room Mother had made so homelike these past three years: glass butterflies in the windows, butterflies on cushions and towels, an indoor garden that was almost a jungle. I stopped at her door, puzzled to find it closed. I knocked. No answer. I forced open the door. "Mother?"

Next moment I froze. Mother's room had been stripped. Every photograph, every houseplant, every butterfly was gone. Only the bare mattress on the bed.

I strode to the nurses' office. "Where have you taken Mother—Helen Sherrill?"

"She's on the Second. I'm sorry."

On the second floor? I headed for the stairs. "Second" was the skilled-care unit, where Mother had gone after the fall that so abruptly ended her independence four years ago. She'd hated it there. Stubbornly, doggedly, against every prognosis, she'd battled mental and physical complications until, fifteen months later, she'd "graduated" down to First. What made them think she couldn't do that again? What did they mean by moving her things out of her room?

"I'm John Sherrill," I said to one of the second-floor staff nurses. "Which is Mother's room, please?"

"Room 245," she told me, and added the same words I'd heard downstairs: "I'm sorry."

Mother's companion, Cennie McClure, dressed in her usual white polyester jacket and slacks, was coming out of Room 245 as I approached. Plump, bright, Cennie was one of the people I most looked forward to seeing on my regular visits from New York. This time, though, Cennie's eyes were tear-swollen. "Be prepared, John," she said as she led me into the white-curtained room.

Although I had seen Mother only three weeks before, I almost did not recognize the thin figure behind the raised bars of the bed. Mother lay under a cotton blanket, eyes closed, head thrashing ceaselessly from side to side. Above her, hanging from metal stands, were upside-down bottles of liquid. Plastic tubing led from the bottles to IVs in Mother's arms.

"Mother?" No response. "Mother, it's Johnny." I used my childhood name, though I was fifty-seven years old myself. "I'm back from Hong Kong." Mother did not open her eyes or slow her tormented tossing. I reached down to take her hand.

And then with a shudder I saw that Mother's wrists were tied to the cotlike metal railings. Feebly, feebly, Mother tugged at the bands of gauze that held her. Once, at school,

I'd seen a butterfly that had been pinned, still fluttering, to a specimen board. . . .

Cennie and I stepped out into the corridor. "About two weeks ago," Cennie said, "your Mother suddenly began to sleep twelve or fourteen hours a day. Her appetite vanished. I would wheel her into the dining room, where she would shove her food around like a kid who doesn't like carrots."

At the same time she started talking about death. "Not fearfully," Cennie said. "Almost as though she were speaking of a friend."

"Four or five days ago," she went on, "your mother came down with pneumonia." This time, unlike her previous illnesses at the Terrace, when she'd eagerly sought medical help, she declined all medication, even refusing to swallow water. The day before yesterday she slipped into a coma. That's when they had brought her up here and commenced intravenous feeding and antibiotics.

"But why tie her down to do it?"

"They had to," Cennie said. "Otherwise, the minute they got the needle in, she'd jerk it out."

That was Mother, all right! Never any doubt where she stood on an issue.

That's when I remembered the Living Will.

The Will was a document Mother had written out some ten years earlier, specifying that if she should ever become terminally ill and at the same time mentally incapacitated and unable to speak for herself, and if in qualified medical opinion the physical condition was irreversible, doctors were to "discontinue all supportive measures for prolonging life." When Mother sent my sister Mary and me copies of this will, neither of us paid much attention. Of *course* no senile old person would want her death dragged out by machines and chemicals and tubes.

But now? A band of fear tightened across my forehead. Were we at this very juncture? Now that "supportive measures" were all that stood between my mother and . . .

I walked uncertainly to the second-floor nurses' office. The name badge on the staff nurse's uniform said "Mrs. Brady."

"Isn't there some way we can make her more comfortable?" I asked. "She hates being shackled that way."

Mrs. Brady's attitude was in keeping with the compassion I'd come to expect at the Terrace. "Maybe you'd like to speak to Dr. Haller?" She handed me the desk telephone and a slip of paper with the number of the Terrace's visiting doctor. Dr. Haller explained that antibiotics were the automatic medical response to pneumonia. As for tying her to the bed: "There's no other way we can get nourishment and medicine into her."

I asked whether he knew that Mother had written out a Living Will. He said that he'd not been aware of that. I asked a lot of other questions, stalling for time. "What would happen," I said at last, my throat tightening, "if you took the needles out?"

Dr. Haller's voice was neither shocked nor reproachful. "Your mother," he said, "would go ahead with her death."

I was digesting that in the pit of my stomach while at the same time a Bible verse was passing through my mind: There is "a time to die" (Ecclesiastes 3:2).

"Nobody," Dr. Haller was saying, "dies of 'old age,'" but always of something specific. Pneumonia is one of the kinder ways—relatively swift and painless. Doctors call it 'the old man's friend.'"

He outlined the steps necessary for the removal of the IVs. Around me the routine sounds of the nursing home went on. A loudspeaker paged a nurse. From her wheelchair an aged woman called over and over for someone named Paul.

Next day and a million phone calls later I was dialing Dr. Haller again. So much had happened since our last talk. I'd obtained another medical opinion. I'd contacted every available member of the family, including Tib, far away in Hawaii on a writing assignment, and our children, and my sister Mary and her children. I'd prayed. I'd talked with the staff at the Terrace and with Mother's close friends. Above all, I'd gone back again and again to that white-curtained room on the second floor, asking Mother's unresponsive, thrashing form if she wanted us to honor that will. "If we untie you, Mother, do you know what that means?" Her eyes did not open.

And now the dreadful moment was upon me. I trembled as I told Dr. Haller of our decision to let Mother "go ahead with her death." Yet even as I spoke, I was not sure. Were we taking on a responsibility human beings should not assume? Or had that been done when her unconscious body was hooked up to those bottles? Not one member of our family had objected to honoring Mother's wishes in her will. The one voice I could not be sure I had heard correctly was the only one that really mattered. What did God want? I yearned to know, not just for my family, but for everyone in this uncharted new era when science can keep our bodies breathing almost indefinitely.

At the end of our conversation Dr. Haller spoke to the nurse, who looked at her watch, made entries in her log, and then asked me to follow her. At the highsided bed the nurse bent over Mother, telling her she'd feel a slight sting as the needles came out. No sign that Mother heard. The needles out, the nurse untied the strip of gauze securing her right hand. I expected Mother's free arm to begin flailing since she had never stopped tugging at her bonds since I arrived; but her hand lay quiet at her side. The nurse unknotted the strip on the other side. Instantly the thrashing of head and body ceased, too. Mother's whole being relaxed into the bed.

When the nurse had gone, I bent close. "It's done now, Mother. The IVs are out. But . . ." I looked at the hands lying so peacefully on the hospital blanket, "I don't need to tell you that, do I?"

It was my turn now to be the restless one. I'd given Cennie some much needed time off, but soon grew fidgety just sitting by the bed. With Mother comatose, there seemed no point in talking. Then I remembered that I had my travel Bible with me. I could read to her! I turned to Psalms, Mother's favorite book. "Blessed is the man," I read softly from Psalm 1, "that walketh not in the counsel of the ungodly . . ."

I glanced up. Mother's eyes were wide open!

I jumped to my feet. "Mother?" She made no sound or movement, but her eyes, brilliant blue, looked directly into mine. Scarcely believing what was happening, I sat down and resumed reading: ". . . I lie down and sleep; I wake again, for the Lord sustains me. I am not afraid . . ." (Psalm 3:5-6, RSV).

Each time I looked up, I met those startling blue eyes. They were not full of mental content, but they were not vacant either. What did they remind me of? Boldly now, oblivious of the nursing staff who came in and out, I read on. Some passages were incredibly apt: "Thou hast given me room when I was in distress . . . in peace I will both lie down and sleep . . ." (4:1, 8, RSV).

Nurses entering the room to take Mother's temperature or to turn her were stunned by the phenomenon of her silent, unblinking alertness. For days they had clapped their hands near her ears and shouted her name without the slightest response.

I read on into the afternoon, covering about a third of the Psalms. There continued to be places where the ancient hymns were so appropriate I couldn't believe they had not been written specifically for our situation: "The cords of death encompassed me . . . the snares of death confronted me. In my distress I called upon the Lord . . ." (18:4-6, RSV).

By five o'clock that afternoon I was growing tired and so, I thought, was Mother. Her eyes remained open, but they were heavy now. So I zipped up my travel Bible, told Mother I'd see her in the morning, kissed her, and left. Her eyes followed, undisturbed, peaceful.

As I got into the car I knew what those eyes reminded me of. So intent, so interested, yet without challenge—Mother's eyes were the eyes of a *baby*. I'd seen our children look at Tib and me that way from their cots. You can't get in touch with a baby's mind, but you never doubt his awareness. There was agelessness in Mother's look, just as in a newborn's. The baby is coming from God; Mother was going to God.

I arrived at the Terrace early next morning to find Cennie there ahead of me. "Any change?"

"No. She slept well, but she won't eat much of anything."

I pulled a chair next to the bed. Mother's eyes were closed. They didn't open even when I told her the latest news of her great-granddaughter. I unzipped my Bible. At the first words of Scripture, those blue eyes opened.

"Then it's true," said Cennie softly.

As long as I read, Mother watched me with that baby's alert, accepting gaze. Then when I reached Psalm 51 a startling thing occurred. Unexpectedly, Mother's wide-open eyes filled with tears. I was stunned, for here was the first direct communication. If not with me, then with God. I read the psalm again: "Have mercy upon me, O God . . . according unto the multitude of thy tender mercies blot out my transgressions. Wash me thoroughly from mine iniquity, and cleanse me from my sin" (51:1-2).

Dear Lord, what transgressions did this lady have that she found weighing on her so heavily? Whatever they were they could not have been as devastating as the author's, who wrote the psalm when he had committed both adultery and murder.

But the tears continued flowing, while I gained new insight into the importance of unencumbered death. If Mother had been fighting life-support systems, she would not have had the internal leisure for the work she was now tackling. This was the "business of dying" people speak about. It was a happening, a rounding off. I found myself praying that my own leave-taking would be as natural.

I knew, of course, that not every end could be so graceful; there is, after all, sudden death, pain-wracked death. But I felt a conviction growing that if any of us has a chance for a natural death in the fullness of old age, he should not have the experience taken away by wires and drugs or other well-meant intrusions.

The following day was the last one I spent with Mother. My sister Mary would be down from Washington to take up the bedside vigil.

I didn't start reading immediately, that third day. All morning I chatted—sometimes with Cennie, then with Mother—although Mother remained in an apparent coma, eyes closed, stirring. The lunch tray came, but she only tasted the food Cennie and I pressed to her lips.

"Well, Mother," I said that afternoon after Cennie left,

"it's time for our last reading." I moved the Bible's zipper along its track, picked up where I had stopped the day before, and started reading. I was afraid to look up, afraid to pursue the marvel of wakefulness too far. Mother had not opened her eyes once today, no matter how much noise or how many people were in the room. At last, midsentence, I glanced toward her.

Mother's eyes were looking straight at me. Wide open, unblinking, overwhelmingly aware.

I came to the final five psalms. Phrases stood out because they described events I was seeing before my eyes: "The Lord sets the prisoners free; the Lord opens the eyes of the blind . . ." (146:7-8, RSV); "Praise the Lord! . . . Praise Him in His mighty firmament! Praise Him for His mighty deeds . . ." (150:1-2, RSV).

I started to close the book, but instead I took Mother's hand in mine. I looked into those unblinking eyes, hoping that at this last moment Mother might squeeze my hand. But that did not happen. Never mind. She was already where I could not follow, in a realm where Spirit spoke to spirit.

I flipped back through the pages and read: "The Lord is my shepherd; I shall not want. He maketh me to lie down in green pastures; he leadeth me beside the still waters . . . Yea, though I walk through the valley of the shadow of death, I will fear no evil; for thou art with me . . . Surely goodness and mercy shall follow me all the days of my life; and I will dwell in the house of the Lord forever" (23:1-2, 4, 6).

Now I closed the book. I kissed Mother on the forehead and left the room. Mary was at her side when she died three days later without opening her eyes again.

John